Antidotes for Healing the Human Body

~ The Complete Version ~

Understanding the Root Causes of Sickness and Disease

Divine Laws for Spiritual Health

TARA CRITCHLEY

WESTBOW
PRESS®
A DIVISION OF THOMAS NELSON
& ZONDERVAN

WestBow Press books may be ordered through booksellers or by contacting:

WestBow Press
A Division of Thomas Nelson & Zondervan
1663 Liberty Drive
Bloomington, IN 47403
www.westbowpress.com
1 (866) 928-1240

Cover artistry and illustrations by Darcy Adams.
Cover background by erikallison.com

Scripture taken from the King James Version of the Bible.

Scripture quotations marked (TLB) are taken from The Living Bible copyright © 1971. Used by permission of Tyndale House Publishers, Inc., Carol Stream, Illinois 60188. All rights reserved.

Text from *The Human Body* reproduced by permission of DK, a division of Penguin Random House, LLC. Copyright © 1995 Dorling Kindersley Limited.

Text from *The Human Body Book* reproduced by permission of DK, a division of Penguin Random House, LLC. Copyright © 2007 Dorling Kindersley Limited.

ISBN: 978-1-9736-0822-6 (sc)
ISBN: 978-1-9736-0824-0 (hc)
ISBN: 978-1-9736-0823-3 (e)

Library of Congress Control Number: 2017917972

Print information available on the last page.

WestBow Press rev. date: 1/15/2018

In loving memory of
my late Bible teachers:
two great lights.

Disease and health, like circumstances,
are rooted in thought.
Sickly thoughts will express themselves
in a sickly body.
Anxiety quickly demoralizes the whole body,
and lays it open to the entrance of disease;
while impure thoughts,
even if not physically indulged,
will soon shatter the nervous system.
Men will continue to have
impure and poisoned blood,
so long as they propagate unclean thoughts.
Change of diet will not help a man
who will not change his thoughts.
When a man makes his thoughts pure,
he no longer desires impure food.
Out of a clean heart
comes a clean life and a clean body.
If you would perfect your body,
guard your mind.

—James Allen, *As a Man Thinketh*

Acknowledgments

The ideas contained in this book were taught to me through the years by my Bible teachers, who have since passed away. What made them extraordinary was the fact that they practiced what they preached and restored the meaning and power of Jesus's message in a way I had never heard before. Their lives gave meaning to mine and left me with a living example of how to walk as Jesus did. I wanted to keep that truth alive so that it could be passed down to my grandchildren, my great-grandchildren, and those who have a love for truth to be an aid for spirituality, health, and well-being.

I would like to thank God for His inspiration in writing this book. This inspiration kept me going to its completion. Since writing these thoughts, I have found my own voice and am grateful for the opportunity to share what I have learned.

I would like to thank my husband, Mark, and my friend, Hannah, for their support, patience and editing help; Darcy for her illustrations; my son, Pagiel, for his writing expertise, and WestBow Press for getting this book out to those who love the truth.

Contents

Introduction

Behavior is an integral part of our health that affects all of our bodily functions. This is confirmed in the scriptures and by many mind-body studies. These studies prove that the way we think and feel affects our health and immune system. The thoughts we think and the choices we make on a daily basis have a direct impact upon us. They send messages via our nervous systems throughout our bodies, affecting every part. It says in Proverbs that as a man thinks in his heart, so is he.[1] How we think is what governs our actions and determines our physical state of being. We can say then that the state of our body reflects the quality of our thoughts. So it would follow that if we have disharmonies in our bodies, thoughts have produced them, whether by lifestyle habits, hereditary influences, or by being drawn to us from some environmental cause.

We are constantly sowing the seeds of our thoughts and emotions. If these are good, we bring forth good fruit. If these are negative, we bring forth bad fruit. This fruit is reflected in our bodies, for it is a portrait of our minds and hearts.

Our attitude draws to us situations to help us see ourselves. God uses these outside circumstances to show us something that we need to see because at that time, it is the most beneficial for our growth. The scriptures remind us, "A man can receive nothing, except it be given him from heaven."[2] That is because God is always in control of our lives. He allows these situations to happen for our good so that we can see a part of ourselves from a higher perspective. Each situation contains valuable messages for us to learn. If we decode these messages with the truth, we can begin to claim the God-given power that resides within each of us. Truth is the most powerful antidote and was given to us by a loving

Father. We can best utilize it by taking charge of our behavior, which will unlock the power that is instilled within us.

The necessity of changing our behavior was confirmed by Jesus when He said to the lame man who He healed, "Sin no more, lest a worse thing come unto thee."[3] This, in effect, tells us that sin caused the man's lame condition. Sin is the refusal to listen to our conscience and apply the principles of truth that we have been made aware of. It is defined in scripture as knowing to do good but not doing it. Sin can be caused by a free-will decision or inherited from a parent or ancestor. When we act on it, it becomes a part of our life. Jesus informed the lame man that if he were to continue in his present lifestyle, it would counteract his present, healed condition. Jesus lovingly brought to light the fact that his behavior caused the lameness. In effect, changing his behavior would not only allow his healing to remain, but it would prevent a worse condition from happening. This conveys the power that the Word of God has to heal when it is applied into life.

The reverse is also true. When its application is denied, a worse condition is created. Our decisions make our conditions better, or they make them worse. The mind is a very powerful tool.

God can heal us, but His willingness is dependent upon our faith in Him. This element of faith is what initiates His healing power. Jesus said to a blind man that He healed, "Thy faith hath made thee whole."[4] This man's faith was necessary in order for Jesus to heal him. Permanent healing is dependent upon our faith and our willpower to change what we have called good.

God is the standard for what is good. What we call good and what He calls good may be two different things. The scripture clarifies this in Proverbs where it says, "There is a way which seemeth right unto a man, but the end thereof are the ways of death."[5] If we live only by our own standards and don't evaluate them with God's principles, we unknowingly head down the wrong path. If we never consider how God feels about the standards we hold, it may bring us down the road of sickness and disease, until we get the message. Our standards are something to reconsider when we are bombarded with physical maladies. When sickness or disease comes upon us, we innately ask ourselves, "Why did this happen to me?" By understanding the spiritual causes, we can probe into the higher meanings of these conditions and discover the answer to this question.

God wants to live within us fully. He does this through our cooperation with His life-giving principles. His promise to those who do this is that He will send His angels to provide divine protection. When God makes a promise, He never breaks it.

"Because thou hast made the LORD,
which is my refuge,
even the most High, thy habitation;
there shall no evil befall thee,
neither shall any plague come nigh thy dwelling.
For he shall give his angels charge over thee,
to keep thee in all thy ways."[6]

We can claim the power of such health-giving promises and protection; however, the offer is conditional. A change in our actions is what produces long-term healing. By transforming our behavior, we can be protected from illness and hereditary influences. Our free will was given to us so that we can choose the right path in order to receive the blessings of health and life. God wants permanent change so that we can become like Him, which will make us happier in this world and the next. The Lord in His humanity came to offer us principles to live by so that while we are on earth, we can have the opportunity to change while we still can.

The decisions we make in this life will affect us eternally. In reality, what we love now will continue to stay with us after death. This is because it has become a part of our nature through the choices we have made. If we really knew how these choices would affect us long term, what checks and balances would we put into place now? This is a personal journey that requires honesty and self-evaluation with scriptural principles. If we neglect these principles, we become our own standard. Pride has a clever way of preventing us from seeing things in the light of truth.

Sickness and disease are telltale signs that it is time for us to make changes in our lives. The messages contained in the disharmonies of our body also contain our answers. Knowing that our ways and standards can be the cause of our own illnesses, we can begin to take a second look at our lives. Observing our patterns of behavior that are in direct conflict with God's commandments is the first step that can bring us back into alignment with God and restore healing energies. By identifying these patterns, we will discover the personal antidotes to apply.

Behavioral change takes time. It takes perseverance to make these changes our own. Jesus put it this way: "If ye continue in my word, *then* are ye my disciples in deed; and ye shall know the truth, and the truth shall make you free."[7] It is this stick-to-itiveness that frees us, no matter what the natural evidence appears to be saying. Our character can develop into a priceless gem when we strive to make God's nature our own.

It is extremely important to focus ahead and not on the condemning voices of the past when making serious changes. We all make mistakes in trying to come out of the behavioral ruts that we have created, and beating ourselves up is part of the problem. If we look at ourselves kindly, as we would look at someone else we love and want to help, we will be able to grow. Our intention is what God looks at and not our mistakes. Self-forgiveness is a necessary element of progress.

I am not negating the fact that we will need medical care when necessary. I believe the greatest good can be accomplished when those in the medical and health fields combine their knowledge with the mind-body sciences. I feel this is the best way to assist people in their healing. When the spirit is healed, the body follows suit.

We cannot be healed internally when the spirit remains sick, for in some degree, we are in a state of separation from the love of God. This separation comes from our own choosing. God allows us to make the choice to live with Him by keeping His principles. If we live without Him by denying His divine laws, we will not be happy with the eternal results. It's up to us.

Much of the medical world is in denial of this behavioral aspect of healing. That is because there is a big industry giant out there. Taking a pill to avoid the pain masks the original problem by giving a quick and sometimes harmful fix, preventing us from probing deeper into our lives. If we lend ourselves only to this avenue of cure, the true cause for illness is never dealt with from the spiritual root. This book is designed to begin the process of healing through the knowledge of spiritual correspondences to counteract that problem. Truth from the scripture is freely given and gives us insight into the meanings of illness.

Spiritual correspondence looks at the natural functions of the body parts to determine their deeper meanings. In this way, we can identify the spiritual causes of our illnesses. By targeting them, we can begin to resolve our emotions and change the behavior that is creating internal damage. Related Bible stories and applications that Jesus gave will help us discover the antidotes for healing our spirit and body.

This book is written with a backdrop of the Ten Commandments. These divine laws keep our body and spirit in alignment with God. Each commandment governs specific parts of the body and is covered chapter by chapter. The related body parts of each commandment are shown in the drawing which precedes each chapter. Above each drawing are the positive qualities that are developed as the commandment is kept. Within each chapter are the antidotes for the ailments that coincide with that commandment. Behavioral changes can be made by applying these antidotes, which are presented through Old Testament stories and the commandments of Jesus.

Antidotes are like hidden gems that contain priceless remedies for us to uncover. These remedies are revealed to us individually through personal introspection, meditation, and divine inspiration. Discovering our personal remedy provides us with a way out of our past habits and behaviors. We can then create new behaviors through the revealed application. This is how health and healing become activated within us.

When new truth is presented, it will always be confronted by reactions from our normal ways and ideas. These reactions resist change. The Spirit of life is ever moving and urges us forward past these reactions to become more like God. You may have never heard the concepts expressed in this book, but my hope is that you will have an open mind to see things in a new light that may forever change the way you live. ☺

Chapter 1

The Ten Commandments

"Fear God, and keep his commandments:
for this is the whole duty of man.
For God shall bring every work into judgment,
with every secret thing, whether it be good,
or whether it be evil."
Ecclesiastes 12:13b–14

The Ten Commandments were given by God to Moses for the children of Israel on Mount Sinai. They are recorded in Exodus 20:2–17 and Deuteronomy 5:6–21. Our country's laws were originally founded on these Ten Commandment principles, which were divine laws to help reestablish heaven on earth. Many of the decisions made by the Founding Fathers took God's laws into account when they established our government. This was so because as God-fearing men, they recognized the serious business of implementing their faith and scriptural principles in public and private life. This enabled us to receive God's blessings as a nation. Our present educational system in America was founded upon the knowledge of God as its basis for being in existence.

Laws have changed since, and new laws have replaced these foundational principles, prohibiting the acknowledgment of God's values and truths in public life. Because these ancient landmarks are being removed, what we are seeing today are the consequential effects spiraling us down into a troublous time. When we desert God and His laws in our public and private life, what can we expect as a nation?

The scriptures teach us that if we refuse God's commandments in private and public living, the blessings of God are removed. The results can be a sickness or disease, the collapse of a society, or the downfall of a nation. This can usher in devastating effects upon us as individuals, the land, or our economy. We are seeing this happen with great intensity today. The values and standards of righteous living have been rapidly eroding.

We are also seeing that many churches no longer deem it necessary to keep the Ten Commandments or the commandments of Jesus as a prerequisite for heavenly life. It is now very much in vogue to believe that Jesus did it all, without any personal responsibility to keep His commandments. This is very contrary to what Jesus taught and to the principles in the Old and New Testaments. The Bible warned us this would happen with greater intensity as people continue to substitute His truths with church doctrines and traditions. This has created a "famine" for hearing the Word of God. A warning was given in the book of Revelation never to add or take away anything that has been written in the scriptures without consequences. This is happening right in front of our eyes, producing imbalances and extremes that will affect us in every avenue of our present-day lives. God will allow this time to run its full course for the greater good for planet earth.

There are consequences for rejecting God's laws in life. The fruit of our own thoughts is what creates it. As it says in the Old Testament, "Stand ye in the ways, and see, and ask for the old paths, where is the good way, and walk therein, and ye shall find rest for your souls. But they said, We will not walk therein ... Hear, O earth: behold, I will bring evil upon this people, even the fruit of their thoughts, because they have not hearkened unto my words, nor to my law, but rejected it."[8] God takes no pleasure in the hurt of anyone. He gives us our own way to teach and correct us, sometimes with devastating effects, hoping we will get the message.

After the 9/11 bombing of the Twin Towers, the reality of the time that we were living in struck me with intensity. I wrote down my thoughts, which were published in the *Record Journal*, titled "Blessings," on October 2, 2001:

We were all hurt by the massive destruction when the towers fell. But God's hurt cries louder than ours when we say we are a just nation under God, as we lie to ourselves and break His laws in every institution we set up. Have we become a nation 'under God' and yet do nothing to allow ourselves to live under His laws? This was not the purpose for our God-given liberty. Yet, even in our pulpits, many of our ministers will not uphold God's laws for fear of the outcry of their congregations. God's heart is broken because of the ministers who have preached that He allows the breaking of His commandments and that there are no consequences for sinning. How many laws have we passed in our judicial system that justifies the breaking of His commandments, easing ourselves into the lie that there are no consequences for forgetting God? Why do we sit idly by as laws are passed giving our children "the right" to no longer be governed by God's commandments in our school systems and then wonder why the results of forgetting God have produced a breeding ground for violence? The scripture warns us that forgetting God in our lives removes His protection. If we continue to discredit God in our public life, we will see the judgments of God increase in intensity. We cannot continue to govern ourselves by standards that are right in our own eyes, twist the application of scripture to suit our own liking and expect to receive His blessings.

What can we do in a time like this when God is removing His protection from our nation? We can begin by personally developing a relationship with God and making a commitment to keep His laws which provide His protection and are life-giving. Our nation may be entrapping itself by a system of laws that excludes God, but that does not mean that we have to. We have the freedom to implement the truth. By doing this, we can start to change things, beginning with ourselves first: one person at a time.

God has always wanted us to know Him within our own heart.

He wanted His laws written on our hearts so that we would be able to express His feelings and know His thoughts. He wanted outstanding people—lights in a dark world—to represent Him. We can only do this by living and walking as Jesus did, unaffected by the opinions of others. It is a very personal journey. In reality, no one can know God's will for another individual. It can only be revealed personally by following His inspiration and His commandments.

If we believe that Jesus did it all and that we have no other responsibility to God, this is not true faith. It does not take faith to believe that someone else did it. This is historical belief. True faith is reflected in the fact that we are a living example of what we believe. It says in James, "Ye see then how that by works a man is justified, and not by faith only."[9] Faith and action have to be combined for God's Word to have an effect in our lives and produce the necessary healing fruit. The truth from the Word of God is a wonderful gift, and we should use it.

Jesus's words and life always encouraged Ten Commandment living. They were the foundation for everything that He said and did. His presence promoted healing and wholeness to everyone that He came in contact with. When a young man asked Him how he could enter heaven after death, Jesus said, "If thou wilt enter into life, keep the commandments."[10] The commandments discipline the inner "man" so that our life can be prepared for a heavenly life.

Contrary to present beliefs and doctrines, one cannot enter heaven without a life according to the commandments. This idea is confirmed in 1 John, where it says, "He that saith, I know him, and keepeth not his commandments, is a liar, and the truth is not in him."[11] We cannot know God without keeping His commandments. The commandments are life and health to our bodies and spirits. When our bodies and minds are in accordance with them, our bodies' systems operate in the divine order for which they were created. It is written in Exodus:

"If thou wilt diligently hearken
to the voice of the LORD thy God,
and wilt do that which is right in his sight,
and wilt give ear to his commandments,
and keep all his statutes,

I will put none of these diseases upon thee ...
for I am the LORD that healeth thee."[12]

The secret here is doing what is right in God's sight. How would we be able to do this unless we knew what His commandments were? Finding out what they really mean from Jesus's perspective and practicing them is what produces life and health.

Jesus taught and lived on a spiritual level. He spoke about the natural things in the world by conveying their spiritual meanings. We can do the same by using spiritual correspondence as a tool to help uncover the spiritual causes of our health problems. The following chapter will give us more insight on spiritual correspondences, what they are, and how we can apply them.

Chapter 2

Spiritual Correspondences

Everything in this natural world has a spiritual meaning, for nothing truly natural can exist without its spiritual counterpart. Even though the natural world appears separate from the spiritual world, they are both linked together. When God created all that He did, His objective was to bring His living, spiritual realities into the natural world. He wanted to produce heaven on earth by having a living relationship with the man and woman He created. His greatest need and desire for planet earth was for mankind to reciprocate their love to Him; by being so in tune with Him in thought, love, and obedience to His Word, they would have power over everything created in the natural world and assist Him in restoring heavenly life to planet earth.

When He created the natural world, He spoke through His Word, and His Spirit materialized His thoughts through creation, flowing through it like a divine thread. His living voice permeates throughout it today and speaks to us of His reality. This living voice can speak to us when we experience the wonders, the quietness, and the beauty of nature. It is in the quiet stillness that we can best hear the voice of God which speaks to us.

"The heavens declare the glory of God;
and the firmament sheweth his handywork.
Day unto day uttereth speech,
and night unto night sheweth knowledge.
There is no speech nor language,
where their voice is not heard."[13]

In Romans, we learn that by observing the things that He made, we can discover more about the spiritual things that they represent:

"The invisible things of him
from the creation of the world
are clearly seen, being understood by
the things that are made,
even his eternal power and Godhead,
so that they are without excuse."[14]

The spiritual world is best understood by observing the natural things that God created. In this way, we can discover their spiritual counterparts that uncover corresponding meanings. These meanings help us develop a spiritual mind so that we better understand the things of God and the messages He is revealing to us. This allows us to develop a deeper communication with God in life.

Developing our spiritual mind is the key to maintaining our communication with God. This requires effort because there is a war going on between our natural mind and the spiritual mind, as we can see in the scripture below:

"But the natural man receiveth not
the things of the Spirit of God:
for they are foolishness unto him:
neither can he know them,
because they are spiritually discerned.
But the spiritual man has insight into everything ...
But, strange as it seems, we Christians actually
have within us a portion
of the very thoughts and mind of Christ."[15]

Maintaining a spiritual mind gives us direction, counsel, and balance in life. It keeps us whole, happy, and in a creative state of mind. It does not look at things as they appear to be, but what they can be. When we implement the truth from an elevated perspective, the energy fields in our being are revitalized by a wellspring of life flowing from within us.

Because we are made in the image and likeness of God, every part of our bodies was created to tell us something about His life within us. The scriptures say that God is a man in human form and shape. We have all the body parts just like He does. Just as our natural body has five senses with all these parts, so does our spiritual body and our soul. Our natural body looks like the spiritual one, and the soul body controls the spiritual body. When the natural body separates from our spiritual body upon death, we will find ourselves very much alive in this spiritual body, having its own set of five spiritual senses. What we do in our natural body affects our spiritual body, which we will have forever.

At times when God chooses, the five spiritual senses are opened so that we can see, hear, smell, taste, and touch things that are not in this natural world, but are very real. Children at young ages are attuned to these senses, and God communicates His living realities to them. It is this spiritual mind that is opened to the innocent in heart and those who have a love for the truth. The closer we get to God, the more spiritual we become, and the more in tune we are with these spiritual senses. We are able to see, hear, smell, taste and touch things that are real in the spiritual world but are veiled to the natural mind. We only use a small portion of the mind of God that has been given to us. Spiritual corresponding is a way to exercise these spiritual senses. In this way, our mind becomes elevated out of the natural world, and we become aware of these spiritual realities that are even more real.

Let us begin with the human body. We can find out what the parts of our body mean spiritually by understanding their natural functions. For example, our hands are what we work with, so they correspond to our works. If we have trouble with our hands, we have to look at our works. Another example is our fingers. Our fingers are used to hold things, so they represent the principles that we hold onto and the abilities that we use. Each finger corresponds to one of the Ten Commandments. Starting with the right hand, the thumb is commandment one. The right forefinger is commandment two, and so on. The left thumb is commandment six, ending with the small finger on the left hand being commandment ten. If anything were to happen to any one of these fingers, it would correspond to that particular commandment that we would need to work on in our life.

Figure 2 shows the parts of the body with their correspondences to help us better understand their spiritual meanings and the messages they provide for us, especially if illness or accident happens to them.

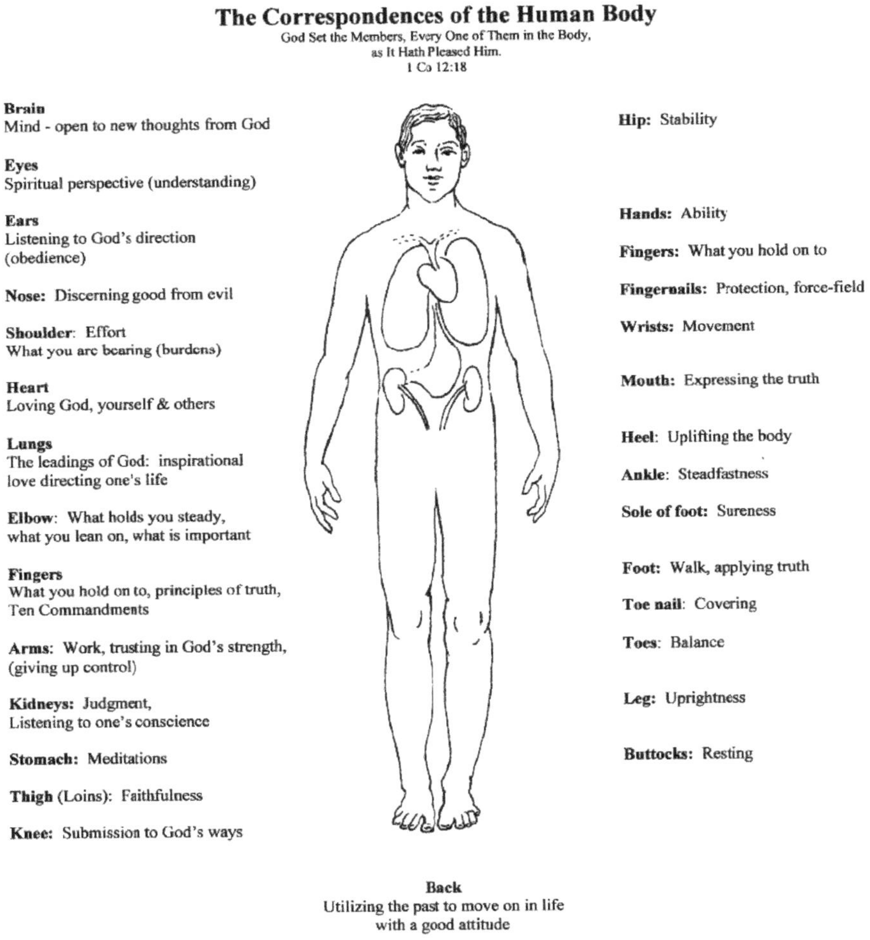

The Correspondences of the Human Body

God Set the Members, Every One of Them in the Body,
as It Hath Pleased Him.
1 Co 12:18

Brain
Mind - open to new thoughts from God

Eyes
Spiritual perspective (understanding)

Ears
Listening to God's direction
(obedience)

Nose: Discerning good from evil

Shoulder: Effort
What you are bearing (burdens)

Heart
Loving God, yourself & others

Lungs
The leadings of God: inspirational
love directing one's life

Elbow: What holds you steady,
what you lean on, what is important

Fingers
What you hold on to, principles of truth,
Ten Commandments

Arms: Work, trusting in God's strength,
(giving up control)

Kidneys: Judgment,
Listening to one's conscience

Stomach: Meditations

Thigh (Loins): Faithfulness

Knee: Submission to God's ways

Hip: Stability

Hands: Ability

Fingers: What you hold on to

Fingernails: Protection, force-field

Wrists: Movement

Mouth: Expressing the truth

Heel: Uplifting the body

Ankle: Steadfastness

Sole of foot: Sureness

Foot: Walk, applying truth

Toe nail: Covering

Toes: Balance

Leg: Uprightness

Buttocks: Resting

Back
Utilizing the past to move on in life
with a good attitude

Figure 2

Love God First
The Blood
Every Whit Whole

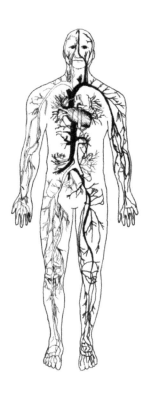

The First Commandment
Figure 3

Chapter 3

The First Commandment

"I am the LORD thy God,
which have brought thee out of the land of Egypt,
out of the house of bondage.
Thou shalt have no other gods before me."
Exodus 20:2–3; Deuteronomy 5:6–7

This commandment makes known the reality of God beginning with the name, I am. This name contains the absolute majesty and omnipotence of an Almighty God who revealed Himself to Moses by speaking to him through a burning bush. God wanted His identity known to the Jewish people, so they would understand the love He had for them. He displayed this when He utilized His omnipotent power through Moses to free them from their bondage to the Egyptians. In doing so, He offered them the opportunity to know Him as God and worship Him. He wanted His love reciprocated and instituted Ten Commandments to help them maintain it. To do this, they had to keep their part of the covenant by keeping His laws. If they did, He would be able to live in and through them, and the blessings of His protection would accompany their life.

Sadly, this love became adulterated. They began to find fault with Him during their circumstances of hardship that He allowed to make them stronger. He had hoped that they would have trusted Him through their difficulties by maintaining a good attitude toward Him.

The few who made it into the Promised Land did so because of their personal vision, despite the opinions of others. Their vision enabled them to see beyond the difficulties and utilize their ingenuity and resourcefulness to partner with God under their circumstances of hardship. Their personal faith in action is what saved them.

God allows certain events in our lives to help us see if we love Him first or find fault with Him. He has control over everything that happens to us and allows it for our eternal good. By drawing from the good qualities deep within ourselves during trying situations, we can bond with God and utilize the strengths He has put within us that help bring us through them.

Job was an example of a man tried by having his livelihood, his family, and his health removed to see if he would maintain his love for God. In the beginning, he did not find fault with his lips, but he did in his heart. The scriptures say that Job was a righteous man. Sometimes, even in our righteousness, pride needs to be exposed so that we can become a better person. Job was one of these men.

Job had a love for truth, which helped him uncover the causes of his health problems. He had boils on his skin, which caused him great pain and heartache for seven years. These boils corresponded to an underlying attitude of pride and self-righteousness that he had not identified in his life, even though he had been serving God. God allowed it to come to a head so that he could see it, get the message, and come up a little higher in his understanding and love for the Lord.

In the ending chapters of Job, he received this revelation when God rebuked him for justifying himself. His love for his own goodness and service had turned into pride, but he had not seen it. This made Job re-evaluate his life and love. When he finally saw the error of his way after years of denial, he repented. God had allowed his three friends to unknowingly demonstrate this pride by the way they spoke to him in their self-righteousness. Now that Job had been humbled and could see himself in God's light, he was able to submit to the Lord with a new love and understanding.

In the end, God changed the captivity of Job when he prayed for his friends. Because Job had gotten the personal message and seen this attitude in his friends as well, he prayed for them with compassion, even though they had caused him so much grief. This helped Job hold no grudges toward God or them for his hard circumstances. Job's realization for the cause of his boils changed his heart and changed his circumstances. After his prayer for his friends, God blessed his life more than at the beginning. His livestock increased, he had ten more children, and he lived a long, healthy life.

Behind every rebuke, heartbreak, illness, calamity, or death, a loving God is there ready to bring us through. Never let go of the eternal bond of trust that you can have with God in this life. Finding the spiritual messages in the things God allows opens a door for us to see His goodness and ultimate purpose. Becoming unveiled to it will change our circumstances. When we see ourselves as God sees us, we can begin our healing process.

In the book *The Power of Positive Thinking,* Norman Vincent Peale found that certain factors were present in successful cases of healing: "First, a complete willingness to surrender oneself into the hands of God. Second, a complete letting go of all error such as sin in any form and a desire to be cleansed in the soul. Third, belief and faith in the combined therapy of medical science in harmony with the healing power of God. Fourth, a sincere willingness to accept God's answer, whatever it may be, and no irritation or bitterness against His will. Fifth, a substantial, unquestioning faith that God can heal."[16]

Healing is a joint effort between us and God, but we must be an active participant for long-term healing to take effect. It takes an open heart and courage to acknowledge the truth about ourselves. As soldiers going to war, we are given the opportunity to slay the negative thoughts and feelings that arise while relying on the Master to guide us through with principle and prayer. It is a delicate operation to identify the bad parts of our nature, which must be removed. Illness gives us this time to rethink our lives. It begins the journey of knowing how to love ourselves as God helps us through the difficulty. Always trust in His loving hand of His goodness, no matter what happens.

It is often stated that it is not given to a man to see himself. We learn about ourselves through the eyes of others and the situations we encounter. Many times, others see what we cannot, or they unknowingly demonstrate by their behavior what we need to see. What we love blinds us to the things that God wants to show us in our lives. When we begin to see ourselves from a higher perspective, we learn how to make amends and work with God to heal ourselves. Illness has a way of defining to us what it is that separates us from the love of God.

Honoring God

> "I am God,
> and there is none else;
> I am God, and there is none like me."[17]

One of the objectives of the first commandment is to honor God for our health and well-being. One way we can apply this is not to bring undue attention to ourselves. God is very child-like. He makes Himself the least obvious for our greatest good, hoping that we find Him. He wants us to be like Him by putting ourselves last. This is the intent of the first commandment.

Jesus's actions gave us an example of how to do this. A certain ruler came up to Jesus and praised Him, "Good Master, what shall I do to inherit eternal life?" And Jesus said unto him, Why callest thou me good? None is good, save one, that is, God."[18] Jesus took no credit to Himself. He gave the attention to God. None of us have any power to do good of ourselves. This only comes from God. We only have the power to choose to do it. No matter how gifted we may be, the gifts are God's to be used for love's sake and not for self-attention. Jesus's example of never accepting credit for the good that He did shows us how serious He was about living this truth.

He also said, "How can ye believe, which receive honour one of another, and seek not the honour that cometh from God only?"[19] When we take a moment and evaluate how many things we do for the sole purpose of gaining attention, we can begin to make changes in these areas in our lives.

Jesus emphasized the fact that no one should lavish undue attention and praise toward another when He said, "Call no man your father upon the earth: for one is your Father, which is in heaven. Neither be ye called masters: for one is your Master, even Christ. But he that is greatest among you shall be your servant. And whosoever shall exalt himself shall be abased; and he that shall humble himself shall be exalted."[20]

The Living Bible puts it this way: "How they enjoy the deference paid them on the streets, and to be called 'Rabbi' and 'Master'! Don't ever let anyone call you that. For only God is your Rabbi and all of you are on the same level, as brothers. The more lowly your service to others, the greater you are. To be the greatest, be a servant."[21] The Lord did not want us to give preferential honor to those who claim they love God but are seeking self-glory. He also instructed us not to follow after their works if their real motive is preventing them from practicing what they preach. The person He uses is only a vessel. The credit should be given to God to whom it is due.

Another way that Jesus put God first in His life was by being a faithful witness to the truth whenever He had an opportunity. When Pilate addressed Him with the fact that he had power to crucify Him or release Him, Jesus's response was that he could have no power at all over Him, unless it was given to him by His Father. Jesus made it clear that God was in control, not Pilate's imagination of himself. Jesus put His trust in God's hands and continued to be faithful, even when faced with His own death. What a vision He had: trusting His Father, who had a higher objective in mind for His life, a pattern for innumerable people to be freed by implementing the truths that He taught. You know that ideas come from God when they honor God first. May it always be in our hearts to seek God's needs before our own so that we can shun the attention-getting desires of our egos. As Jesus reminds us in John:

> "He that speaketh of himself
> seeketh his own glory:
> but he that seeketh his glory that sent him,
> the same is true, and no unrighteousness is in him."[22]

Faith and trust in the reality of God restores the power of God into our lives. These qualities assist in healing our spirits and bodies. Jesus's life portrayed a living example of this reality by restoring the power of God in the lives of those He met. His life so embodied the application of loving God first by living the truth, that His very clothes were an extension of that power of His life. Women were healed of blood diseases just by touching His robe. This was because of their belief in the reality of who He was. He expressed to these women that *their* faith in God is what had made them whole. The Spirit of God in His life activated and confirmed the power of their faith.

The Spiritual Correspondence of the Blood

"For the life of all flesh is in the blood."
Leviticus 17:11a

The blood corresponds to the life of God within us. We could not live without the Spirit of life flowing through our blood. The commandment to love God first governs the blood, for loving God first is the sole purpose of our very life. Jesus clarified this when He said, "And this is life eternal, that they might know thee, the only true God, and Jesus Christ, whom thou hast sent."[23] Life is about knowing who God is. Living His truth taps us into His life-giving energies which purifies our blood and makes us completely whole: every whit.

Only the Spirit of life can reveal the truth about God to anyone. But this Spirit is only given to those who have a desire to live the truth and obey it. When this Spirit becomes captured because of other loves within our hearts, the truth about the existence of God and the necessity of keeping His laws is easily explained away.

"For to be carnally minded is death;
but to be spiritually minded is life and peace.
Because the carnal mind is enmity against God:
for it is not subject to the law of God,
neither indeed can be."[24]

Because the blood scripturally represents the life, Jesus used it in a parable to elevate our understanding of it: "Except ye eat the flesh of the Son of Man, and drink his blood, ye have no life in you."[25] The symbolic terms of eating His flesh and drinking His blood meant that He wanted us to partake of His life by applying His words so that His life would become ours. In this way, we could become like God. We do not obtain His life by repeating the symbolic act. We obtain it by believing in the truth He taught so much that we subject our will to the Father's will in order to obtain eternal life while on the earth. This gives us the power to overcome evil, as He did.

> "As the living Father hath sent me,
> and I live by the Father:
> so he that eateth me,
> even he shall live by me."[26]

Exposing our lives to the divine laws that Jesus taught helps us to identify bad habits and attitudes so that we can replace them with His divine laws and requirements that lead to a heavenly life. As we do this on a daily basis, a "transfusion" is made. By shunning the evils of human nature, the Spirit of God progressively enters us and transforms us in a new and living way.

The Function of the Blood

The job of the blood is to keep the cells healthy and alive. The function of the blood is described in *The Human Body Book* as follows: "Blood delivers oxygen and nutrients to body cells, collects waste, distributes hormones, spreads heat around the body to control temperature, and plays a part in fighting infection and healing injuries. A constant and adequate blood supply is essential for healthy tissues."[27] When our blood is doing its job, our bodies are protected and are able to heal themselves.

All of the blood cells are speaking and communicating within our bodies. Every emotion, every thought, and every situation that we encounter is being recorded in our blood: how we felt, and what we experienced. This is because the Spirit of life, who knows all things, is housed within our blood. Our blood has a voice and is a living essence of all of our emotions and thoughts. We see this revealed in Genesis, when God spoke to Cain, who had murdered his brother, Abel:

> "The voice of thy brother's blood
> crieth unto me from the ground."[28]

Spiritual Causes of Blood Diseases

Untrue ideas about God that have become part of our lives pollute the blood. Denial of God, His laws, and our responsibility to them fill our minds and bodies with error. Blood diseases result because truth is being mixed with error. These diseases can stem from a present mind-set or a past lifestyle, or they can be inherited through the genes from the behaviors of our ancestors, which have become part of our lives.

If blood diseases are inherited, the genes passed down to us contain the character weaknesses of those who have made a lifestyle of denying God through erroneous thinking and behavior. This behavior over time breaks down the genetic structure in our blood line and makes us accessible to it when we succumb to similar attitudes and behaviors in our lives. Living in error allows for self-indulgent behavior; there is no life from God within it. Those who reject God's principles and live contrary to them not only reject God and His life, they unknowingly create within themselves the breakdown of their own immune systems. When good and evil are mixed together, the power of God becomes diluted, resulting in uncleanness that manifests correspondingly as blood diseases. It is the truth that can purge us and produce a greater influx of the Spirit of life within us.

Antidotes for Blood Diseases

Jesus left us an example of how to apply the truth so that we could do it too. Living this way empowers us with a heavenly life. His miracles were a demonstration of what is common in heavenly life, and He demonstrated it to show that it's possible for us to attain it while we are in human flesh on earth. He invited us to follow His pattern by making our natural minds spiritual. We do this by being aware of our choices of good and evil in our daily walk. By shunning evil and error, we find out who God really is, and who we are, as well. We find a treasure that is hidden in our field. This is the reward of a God-centered life. The Spirit of God will progressively lead us out of ego-centered lives into a life of divine usefulness. As the Spirit of wisdom so aptly put in the book of Proverbs,

"Hear instruction, and be wise, and refuse it not.
For whoso findeth me findeth life,
and shall obtain favor of the LORD.
But he that sinneth against me wrongeth his own soul:
all they that hate me love death."[29]

The Spirit of wisdom will transform our minds into spiritual ones by helping us identify what is unlike God within us. When we identify these negative habits, we can use the power of truth to speak to them as a separate entity and cast them out, as Jesus did. He referred to them as devils, demons, and unclean spirits. When He spoke to them, they had to leave, and angels replaced them. In this way, negative life patterns that resulted in sicknesses and diseases were removed, and His life entered people to strengthen and heal them. Putting this truth into practice as Jesus did not only elevates our minds, it also energizes every cell in our bodies, invigorating our blood with life from the Spirit of God. We become clean by implementing Jesus's words, as we are reminded in John:

"Now ye are clean through the word
which I have spoken unto you ...
If ye abide in me, and my words abide in you,
ye shall ask what ye will,
and it shall be done unto you."[30]

Separating error from our lifestyles will help restore the power of God back into our lives and our blood. This is done by looking for areas where we have refused to acknowledge God, His reality, and the application of truth. What areas of our lives do we not want God to be a part of? Addressing them will help us to see the wrong motivations that have been controlling us. Once we see them, we can talk to God about it. By using Jesus's name, we can cast out the negative thoughts and actions and replace them with the opposite, angelic qualities. This will fill us with a greater love for ourselves and the truth. The Word of God has restorative power when error is identified and removed from our lives.

Understanding what is good and evil can only be revealed from the light of truth. When we use the truth to change our negative actions, our spirit (and blood) can be purified from the root. The Lord will then show us the best road to take regarding our natural health care.

"I call heaven and earth to record this day against you,
that I have set before you life and death,
blessing and cursing: therefore choose life,
that both thou and thy seed may live:
that thou mayest love the LORD thy God, and that
thou mayest obey his voice,
and that thou mayest cleave unto him:
for he is thy life, and the length of thy days."[31]

No Images (Idolatry)
Heart and Mind (Senses)
Sanity, Intelligence, and Stability

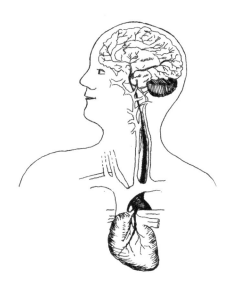

The Second Commandment
Figure 4

Chapter 4

The Second Commandment

"Thou shalt not make unto thee any graven image,
or any likeness of any thing that is in heaven above,
or that is in the earth beneath,
or that is in the water under the earth:
thou shalt not bow down thyself to them, nor serve them:
for I the LORD thy God am a jealous God, visiting the iniquity
of the fathers upon the children unto the third and fourth
generation of them that hate me; and showing mercy unto
thousands of them that love me, and keep my commandments."
Exodus 20:4–6; Deuteronomy 5:8–10

This commandment tells us that we are not to have any idols or graven images before God. This is because in reality, there is only one God, who created us, and He should be worshipped for Himself alone.

Whatever we love above all else becomes a "god" to us. This is an idol that we fashion after the imagination of our own heart. Things that we love before God are never identified as another "god" because our love is in them, preventing us from seeing them as such. This commandment was written to help us identify them. When we love something before God, we use our hearts and minds to pursue it. It would follow then that the health of our hearts and minds are determined by how this commandment has been kept.

If we have heart problems or mental instability, we can know that there is another love that we have before God. It is an image graven upon our hearts and minds because of habitual thoughts, desires, and actions that we have made our own. We can look deep within to find out what these loves may be. It may be our wealth, our reputation, our job, our family, or even ourselves. Actions are usually very telling as to what we love. What we love to spend our time thinking about and doing will give us some clues.

Jesus made it clear that unless God's will and truth are first before anyone or anything in our lives, we cannot be a true disciple. This is necessary so that we can learn to see things from His perspective and develop a love to become like Him that will supersede these loves. Jesus knew that what we loved first would take priority in our lives. He clarified what it meant to not put anyone we love before God in Luke:

> "If any man come to me, and hate not his father,
> and mother, and wife, and children,
> and brethren, and sisters,
> yea, and his own life also,
> he cannot be my disciple."[32]

The word "hate" here does not mean that we are to dislike our families or ourselves. It means that we are to love God more than our father, our mother, our wife, our husband, or family, as well as our own lives. At times, this means that we must make sacrifices apart from our family's wishes in order to accomplish God's purposes in our lives.

Jesus clarified the idea of making God a priority when He said, "No man can serve two masters: for either he will hate the one, and love the other; or else he will hold to the one, and despise the other. Ye cannot serve God and mammon … But seek ye first the kingdom of God, and his righteousness; and all these things shall be added unto you."[33] In this case, Jesus reiterated the fact that we cannot have two priorities, serving money (mammon) and serving God at the same time, for they will conflict. By seeking the kingdom of God first within ourselves, Jesus reassured us that our daily needs would be taken care of. This is a promise which requires trust in God and a refocusing of our priorities. Making money should be secondary to being useful to God as we begin to fill our hearts and minds with love and truth.

No matter how great our natural needs are, when the search for God is first, He will provide for us. I have seen this happen many times in my life. It is a written promise that is dependent upon our desire to search out His will before our own needs. He will always keep His side of the promise and provide for us. When we trust Him this way, we are able to accomplish what He has put us here to do.

The second commandment says that God is a jealous God. He is jealous for our love and wants it for Himself first. In our teenage lives, our first love is very special. This is what God wants from us: a first love that is set apart from any other love. When we love Him this way, we can do the greatest good. Replacing this first love with other desires makes God jealous, for we have another love that we do not want God to touch. This love becomes an idol, for we hold on stubbornly to what we want the most, in place of God.

When idolatry and stubbornness have become our lifestyle, these traits are passed down through our genes to our children, grandchildren, and great-grandchildren. These behaviors result in producing hereditary sicknesses and maladies. This is not God's doing. It is the effect of behavior that has remained undisciplined, passed down through the genes from our hereditary lines.

God has showed mercy to thousands of people who have loved Him and kept His commandments, no matter what hereditary illnesses were present. In many cases, He has healed their conditions because they made their hearts right with Him by removing those things they had put before Him.

Hereditary Disease

Repeated negative behaviors that have become lifestyle habits are door-openers to genetic diseases. Denial of these behaviors keeps us subjugated to them. According to the book *Breaking the Habit of Being Yourself*, "If we stay in the same toxic state of anger, the same melancholy state of depression, the same vigilant state of anxiety, or the same low state of unworthiness, those redundant chemical signals ... keep pushing the same genetic buttons, which ultimately cause the activation of certain diseases. Stressful emotions ... actually pull the genetic trigger, dysregulating the cells … and creating disease. When we … memorize familiar states of being, our internal chemical state keeps activating the same genes, meaning that we keep making the same proteins. But the body cannot adapt to these repeated demands, and it begins to break down."[34] In effect, we may be living someone else's hereditary life in our own lineage and not even know it, since those tendencies in our lives are so strong.

This reality helps us realize that we must change the habits that are running our life, for they create diseases not only within us but in the lives of our children as well. By identifying these patterns, we can apply the truth to change the behaviors that are producing these negative effects. We do this little by little by making better choices on a daily basis.

Illnesses help us address hard issues that we need to face and cause us to come to terms with wrong decisions that we've made. By understanding these causes without condemning ourselves, we can progress toward healing. We can do our part, but the resulting healing always remains in God's hands. We must trust that He has our best interest in mind, whatever the outcome may be. It is all to strengthen our attitude of heart, which will assist in healing our spiritual bodies first. God always looks at the heart but has our greatest eternal good in mind for each situation that He allows. No matter what stage of illness we may be in, if we can work to change for the better by learning what our bodies are telling us, we can begin the healing process. It is our attitude that makes all the difference. It is a fight for our very lives that requires faith and love in a wonderful Creator that can help us override the impossibility of any situation, providing it is His will.

God is a God of the impossible. Shadrach, Meshach, and Abednego said, before they were thrown into a fiery furnace, "Our God whom we serve is able to deliver us from the burning fiery furnace … But if not, be it known unto thee, O king, that we will not serve thy gods, nor worship the golden image which thou hast set up."[35] This is the kind of stamina and determination one must have when facing impossibility. They believed God could do it, but whether He did it or not was God's business. They were able to maintain their stance during this life-threatening situation. What an example of never losing faith in God, even if He chooses not to meet our expectations.

There is a more far-reaching plan for us than what is on this planet.

Our job is to remain true to His principles without finding fault. As Job said through his ordeal with boils, "Though he slay me, yet will I trust in him."[36] We have to trust in God's love to know that no matter what situation we encounter, there is a plan for our eternal good.

Talking with God

God knows our problems before we even express them. When we talk with Him, it sets in motion angels to assist us. In the Living Bible translation of James, we are given insight on how to talk to God: "Is your life full of difficulties and temptations? Then be happy, for when the way is rough, your patience has a chance to grow. So let it grow, and don't try to squirm out of your problems. For when your patience is finally in full bloom, then you will be ready for anything, strong in character, full and complete. If you want to know what God wants you to do, ask him, and he will gladly tell you, for he is always ready to give a bountiful supply of wisdom to all who ask him.... But when you ask him, be sure that you really expect him to tell you, for a doubtful mind will be unsettled as a wave of the sea that is driven and tossed by the wind; and every decision you then make will be uncertain, as you turn first this way, and then that. If you don't ask with faith, don't expect the Lord to give you any solid answer."[37]

When we approach God with a believing heart and expect Him to answer us, He is more than ready to give us counsel and advice. Talking to Him and trusting Him calms our mind, sharpens our five senses, and strengthens our heart.

The Heart

The heart is the pump for all the blood in the body. The power of God keeps our heart beating and our blood flowing so that we can have a healthy body and mind. We should be thankful every day for the small, unobvious wonders that His life provides for us on a daily basis. We should do everything possible to take care of the bodies that He dwells in, naturally and spiritually.

The heart is the seat of love and affection, the place where we feel

God's love. Our heart has the capacity to love without receiving anything in return. This is love in its most selfless form. It is the love that Jesus had for His Father and His fellow man. This kind of love puts God first and gives us the faith to withstand rejection and abuse without succumbing to the hatred of human nature. When we guard the affections of our heart with a love for truth, we add years to our life. Hardening our heart to situations in life because of anger or fear creates blockages that affect the health of our hearts and minds, but if the eye of our hearts remains on God and seeks to resolve angers and fears, our whole body is filled with light and becomes radiant with life-giving energies.

Idolatry's Effect on the Mind and Heart

Anyone who chooses to worship an image of himself or another affects his health in many ways. Idolatry is an unrealistic image or expectation. It hardens our heart to the love of God and often creates an anger that can be explosive when God allows that love to be touched. We may have a set way of doing things, and we do not want to be told differently. This attitude over time affects the heart and mind, for we are putting out energy to maintain an idol in our lives. When we use the heart and mind to block God out because of strong, unregulated emotions, we begin creating problems of emotional and mental instability or heart problems. Our fight creates an overload of stress because another love is in the way. The emotional stress of this love causes us to lose our reasoning and judgment. As a result, the flow of God's energy to our minds and hearts becomes misdirected, overwhelming them and restricting proper blood flow.

The Worship of Angels

When we worship angels or spiritual beings, we replace the worship of God with an idol. John had this experience in the book of Revelation when he was overwhelmed by the presence of an angel. When he saw him, he bowed down to him. The angel instructed him, "See thou do it not: for I am thy fellowservant, and of thy brethren the prophets, and of them which keep the sayings of this book: worship God."[38]

Even the angels know that all praise is to be given to God, for their power lies in honoring Him. Angels are averse to all praise and honor for themselves, for their main joy is their love for God and their usefulness to mankind.

It says in *Heaven and Hell* that "angels have no power whatever from themselves.... Whoever of them believes that he has power from himself instantly becomes so weak as not to be able to resist even a single evil spirit. For this reason angels ascribe no merit whatever to themselves, and are averse to all praise and glory on account of any thing they do, ascribing all the praise and glory to the Lord."[39] Power from God is what gives us strength to our minds and hearts. If angels are doing this, shouldn't we? The next time someone praises you, say, "Thank God" (inwardly or outwardly), for it is only His life that inspires us to do good, and we are only vessels of His goodness.

Spiritual Causes of Heart Problems

Heart problems in general reflect a love that we have placed before God, or the refusal to make our heart right with God. Within our hearts is where deep-seated, unresolved emotions lodge. When these emotions are not addressed, their built-up pressure can lead to imaginary fears, producing unnecessary stress on the heart.

Unresolved emotions must be expressed in order for us to receive clarity about how we think and feel. This can be done by talking with God, a trustworthy friend, or a counselor. It can also be done by writing in a journal to get your feelings on paper. Find a quiet spot and go within and talk to God. Be open to His thoughts and inspirations. His answers might surprise you. As the scriptures say,

> "There is a friend that sticketh closer
> than a brother."[40]

Antidotes for Heart Problems

> "Commune with your own heart upon your bed, and
> be still."[41]

> "Peace I leave with you, my peace I give unto you....
> Let not your heart be troubled, neither let it be afraid."[42]

God's voice provides us with internal peace and comfort, which gives us an assurance to help us overcome our fears.

> "Wait on the LORD: be of good courage, and he shall strengthen thine heart: wait, I say, on the LORD."[43]

> "I cry unto thee, when my heart is overwhelmed: lead me to the rock that is higher than I."[44] When our hearts are inundated by stress, God can unveil our minds to perceive things from a higher perspective.

> "Ye shall be clean: from all your filthiness, and from all your idols, will I cleanse you. A new heart also will I give you, and a new spirit will I put within you: and I will take away the stony heart out of your flesh, and I will give you an heart of flesh. And I will put my spirit within you, and cause you to walk in my statutes, and ye shall keep my judgments, and do them."[45]

When we obey God's voice within, His Spirit removes our hardness and energizes our hearts.

Laughter eliminates stress on the heart. See the bright side of everything. Humor is the elixir of life.

> "A merry heart doeth good like a medicine."[46]

Causes and Antidotes for High Blood Pressure

Our lifestyle habits and the way we handle stress affect our blood pressure. High blood pressure inhibits the circulatory system from flowing freely. In *The Human Body Book,* we see some of the natural causes for high blood pressure: "Lifestyle and genetic factors may contribute, as do being overweight, drinking excessive amounts of alcohol, smoking and having a high-salt diet. A stressful lifestyle may aggravate the condition."[47]

Removing stress-producing fear is helpful and important for lowering blood pressure. Fear has an appearance of reality. Its job is to capture and magnetize our minds to it so that its perception becomes real to us. If we do not accept its reality, it loses power over us. There is nothing wrong with feeling fear, but we master it by staying above it. This is done by dwelling on positive thoughts. When we do this, our perception will change, and so will our circumstances. Look at fearful situations as an eternal benefactor. It's not what happens, but how we take it that matters. God is in control, and knowing this gives us an assurance, no matter what happens. When love is ruling our hearts, fear cannot remain. As it says in Matthew:

> "Thou shalt love the Lord thy God with all thy heart,
> and with all thy soul, and with all thy mind.
> This is the first and great commandment.
> And the second *is* like unto it,
> Thou shalt love thy neighbor as thyself."[48]

Mental Instability

Mental instability is produced when we have other loves before God. These loves restrict God's energies to our brain, creating a loss of reasoning and judgment. Decision making becomes faulty, and we are plagued with fears and obsessions. The scriptures say in James, "A double-minded man is unstable in all his ways."[49]

King Saul and Mental Instability

Saul was an example of one suffering from mental instability. His problem was stubbornness and disobedience to the will of God through the prophet Samuel. When Saul was told by Samuel to slay the Amalekites and all that they had, Saul did what he thought was good in his own eyes and kept the king alive, along with the best of the animals. He did this mainly to please the people. When Saul's behavior was addressed by Samuel, he denied that he had disobeyed God's will because it had become his lifestyle. Pride now dominated his reasoning, and he was no longer listening or in control. Samuel brought his deed to light in 1 Samuel 15, where he said, "Hath the LORD as great delight in burnt offerings and sacrifices, as in obeying the voice of the LORD? Behold, to obey is better than sacrifice, and to hearken than the fat of rams. For rebellion is as the sin of witchcraft, and stubbornness is as iniquity and idolatry. Because thou hast rejected the word of the LORD, he hath also rejected thee from being king."[50] Samuel emphasized the fact that obeying God was more important than position or religious duty. Saul's persistence and stubborn mind-set caused his mental faculties to fail. The Spirit of God, which produces sound reasoning, left him, and the fruit of his stubbornness began to plague him. Saul now lived with an unstable mind.

As we can see, self-love has a way of infusing into our imaginations false images about ourselves. These imaginations inspire us to obey our own desires and please other people, instead of doing what God wants. They fool us into believing that they are true because they foster self-love and pride. Our decisions are no longer based on a love for the truth, and we remain unaware of the danger. Obeying God is what produces a sound mind, but obeying our own desires produces an unstable one.

Spiritual Causes of Mental Instability

We diminish the energy to our minds and senses when we deny or distort the truth or use the knowledge of it for personal glory. When these have become our life through habitual actions, problems with mental instability can develop. God's energies can only flow freely to the brain when the truth in our minds is being utilized for the right reasons. If our fears cause us to avoid implementing what is true, the energy to the brain becomes misdirected which affects our emotional state of mind.

The heart and mind must work in harmony in order for them to be healthy. If one is dominating the other, the health of the mind and heart are affected. In the book *Anatomy of the Spirit,* it says, "If mind and heart are not communicating clearly with each other, one will dominate the other. When our minds are in the lead, we suffer emotionally because we turn emotional data into an enemy. We seek to control all situations and relationships and maintain authority over emotions."[51] The objective here is to get a balance between the heart and mind. The mind must submit to the direction of God's Spirit, and the emotions must follow the direction of God's principles. When they both work together, there is complete harmony, and the energies form a complete circuit. Power accompanies such a life, for both the heart and mind are in agreement with God's thoughts and feelings within ourselves. Following the leadings of God's Spirit must be an integral part of our lives in order to be spiritually whole and healthy.

There are many kinds of mental illnesses. Some are more severe than others, depending upon the depth of the denial. Anxiety states and neurosis reflect a fear that prevents us from seeing ourselves in the light of truth. It is a fear that comes when we cannot bring ourselves to address our feelings; therefore, we begin to create an alternate reality. The continual avoidance of these feelings overwhelms the nervous system and begins to affect the mind. We lose touch with ourselves because we have lost touch with God in our lives.

Antidotes for Mental Instability

"There is no fear in love; but perfect love casteth out fear."[52]

"For God hath not given us the spirit of fear; but of power, and of love, and of a sound mind."[53]

The Spirit of God brings us into situations to address our fears so that we will allow God to walk us through them without succumbing to them.

"But the wisdom that is from above is first pure, then peaceable, gentle, and easy to be intreated, full of mercy and good fruits, without partiality, and without hypocrisy. And the fruit of righteousness is sown in peace of them that make peace."[54]

God inspires us with the wisdom to have an entreatable mind when seeing ourselves. When we are honest about our faults, wisdom gives us the proper direction go.

> "Thou wilt keep him in perfect peace, whose mind is stayed on thee: because he trusteth in thee."[55]

> "And be not conformed to this world: but be ye transformed by the renewing of your mind, that ye may prove what is that good, and acceptable, and perfect, will of God."[56]

Thou Shalt Not Take the Name of the Lord thy God in Vain
Mouth, Throat, and Teeth
Good Manners and Speech

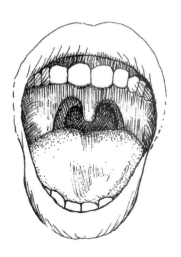

The Third Commandment
Figure 5

Chapter 5

The Third Commandment

"Thou shalt not take the name of the LORD thy God in vain;
for the LORD will not hold him guiltless
that taketh his name in vain."
Exodus 20:7; Deuteronomy 5:11

This commandment states that we should not use the name of the Lord with disrespect. The word "vain" in the Hebrew means a false way or destructively. A name depicts one's character. By using God's name this way, we dishonor His character and His life. As the commandment says, we are held accountable for misusing it.

This commandment was written with our eternal good in mind so that we would curb our verbal actions to honor God. When we verbalize respect for God, power flows freely within our being to keep our mouth and throat healthy. If we misrepresent Him or falsify the truth that we know, the power to our mouth and throat becomes diminished, leaving them open to health problems. What happens to our mouth and throat is caused by vocalizing in a false way.

How do we take God's name in vain? When we use it to curse or degrade, for we are justifying our frustration and using God's name to enforce it. By misusing His name in moments of heated anger, we are validating negative thoughts. We may feel empowered, but we are actually losing power when we do this. As God says in Isaiah, "So are my ways higher than your ways, and my thoughts than your thoughts."[57] Therefore, we should think twice before attributing evil to Him.

The Serpent on the Pole

The following story in Numbers 21 shows how a negative attitude toward God or His servants can create a troubling situation. The children of Israel became discouraged in the wilderness and began to find fault with Moses. They had to eat manna, which they hated. This light bread was miraculously provided by God for their survival. Instead of having a good attitude about the kind of food they were given, they belittled God and Moses for not giving them what they wanted. Their biting tongue began to manifest as fiery serpents that appeared, biting and killing many of them. After this event, God instructed Moses to make a serpent of brass so that those who had been bitten could look upon it and be healed. This method required that they honor God's voice in Moses and take a good look at the serpent in their heart. The children of Israel had to come to terms with their biting attitude. By doing these things, many of their lives were saved, and they were healed.

This serpent on the pole has become the symbol of the medical profession, a token of healing. It also continues to hold a valuable lesson for us to see ourselves as God sees us, for this is what begins our healing process. Life is our teacher, and the attitude that we maintain determines the quality of the person that we will be forever. By taking a good look at what is killing us, we have an opportunity to find the cause and be healed: a life for a look.

Serpent on the pole
Figure 6

Mouth and Throat

> "Who hath made man's mouth …
> have not I, the LORD?
> Now therefore go, and I will be with thy mouth,
> and teach thee what thou shalt say."[58]

Our tongue is a very small member of our body, yet it has the monumental job of directing our course by what we say. The scripture likens the tongue to a rudder on a ship's helm, which is able to turn around the entire ship, and a bridle in a horse's mouth, which is able to turn around its whole body.

The tongue can be unruly and can "run on and on" without a thought. Words spoken without thinking can cause a lot of trouble. How many times did we wish that we hadn't said that? Sometimes, it is better to hold our tongue and think before we speak.

We cannot claim to be a lover of God and not discipline what comes out of our mouth. Discipline is a necessary element to curb human nature; otherwise, the tongue will continue establishing its own standards and voicing them to protect the selfish life.

> "Anyone who says he is a Christian
> but doesn't control his sharp tongue
> is just fooling himself,
> and his religion isn't worth much."[59]

We learn what is in our heart by what comes out of our mouth: what we say and how we say it. It is a study in itself. Jesus said that it is not what we put into our mouth that causes us to become unclean but what comes out of it. This shows us the weight that our words have on producing unclean and unhealthy conditions.

We create unclean conditions in our spirit body first, for this is the house of our thoughts. Jesus often addressed behavior in this realm, for thoughts are very much alive in the spirit world. Jesus answered the thoughts of people before they expressed them. He could hear them and knew what people were really thinking and planning.

If we do not change the negative thoughts that we are dwelling upon, they will eventually affect our actions and our health. Our conscience was given so we could weed out these bad thoughts and actions. If we do not do this, their damaging effects will begin to manifest in our bodies. This occurs especially in the area of misuse. It is as if we create a blueprint from our thoughts and actions on the body parts that we are misusing. Because of these wrong desires, we draw to ourselves sicknesses or accidents that affect these areas. This is why it is important for us to control our tongue. We are sons and daughters of a living, creative God. We have power in our words to create good or evil.

> "Death and life are in the power of the tongue:
> and they that love it
> shall eat the fruit thereof." [60]

A man's word used to mean something. It was a bond, a commitment to do what was said because men were true to their beliefs. There were no signed contracts like today. People's words today have become meaningless in the trust department and must be legally enforced on paper, so they will be believed. Trust is only developed when people repeatedly keep their words and commitments; then, their words are trustworthy because their life is behind them. It is this kind of living that produces a heavenly nature. It is hard to find righteous people today who really mean what they say and say what they mean. This is very reflective of the times that we are living in.

Religious Hypocrisy

> "This people draw near me with their mouth,
> and with their lips do honour me,
> but have removed their heart far from me,
> and their fear toward me
> is taught by the precept of men." [61]

It is hurtful to God in our lives when we use our mouth to say one thing and do another, especially when we claim to love Him. We may be able to get away with being two-faced down here, but in reality, we are only fooling ourselves. A life of hypocrisy created here will follow us after death. There, we will not be able to change what has become our life. In the spirit world, if we try to say one thing and do another, our real intention will be revealed, for our deeds will come alive to show us to ourselves. It is better for us to be as real and true as we can now so that this lifestyle will follow us after death. Otherwise, we may be surprised to find out that our superficial vocalizing about our love for God will never keep us from going to where our behavior will eventually take us.

Spiritual Causes of Mouth and Throat Problems

When we begin venting accusations on a habitual basis, impairments of the mouth and throat are set in motion in spirit. Mouth sores, cankers, and gum infections are caused by the following: taking God's name in vain, falsely accusing someone, running down another's character, or speaking evil of the truth. Causes of throat problems include lying, gossiping, refusing to confess, and not speaking up to defend an innocent person.

Antidotes for Mouth and Throat Problems

The energies that protect the throat work in a harmonious flow when we vocalize what is true about God, ourselves, and others. Mouth and throat problems can be healed by admitting we were wrong and speaking what is true and good.

> "Teach me, and I will hold my tongue: and cause me to understand wherein I have erred."[62]

> "The tongue of the wise is health."[63]

Speak out against someone you know who is doing the wrong thing. If you know about it and do not say anything, you are just as guilty, for your silence condones their actions.

> "Telling the truth gives a man great satisfaction and hard work returns many blessings to him. A fool thinks he

43

needs no advice, but a wise man listens to others. A fool is quick-tempered; a wise man stays cool when insulted. A good man is known by his truthfulness; a false man by deceit and lies. Some people like to make cutting remarks, but the words of the wise soothe and heal. Truth stands the test of time; lies are soon exposed."[64]

"Don't talk so much. You keep putting your foot in your mouth. Be sensible and turn off the flow! When a good man speaks, he is worth listening to, but the words of fools are a dime a dozen."[65]

"The lips of the righteous feed many: but fools die for want of wisdom."[66]

"Do you want a long, good life? Then watch your tongue! Keep your lips from lying. Turn from all known sin and spend your time in doing good. Try to live in peace with everyone; work hard at it."[67]

"Be not rash with thy mouth, and let not thine heart be hasty to utter any thing before God: for God is in heaven, and thou upon earth: therefore let thy words be few."[68]

"Let your speech be always with grace, seasoned with salt, that ye may know how ye ought to answer every man."[69]

Salt is a natural healing remedy for the mouth, gums, and throat. Salt spiritually represents the truth, and truth spoken in season is a healing element for the natural and spiritual bodies.

Spiritual Correspondence of the Teeth

The teeth correspond to principles of truth, because they are a part of the bone structure of our mouth. This is because the truth is the foundation for our spiritual house or body, just as the bones are the foundation for our natural body. According to John Worcester in *Physiological Correspondences,* "People in the other life who lack spiritual intelligence and charity, by not having made the truth useful in their lives, are correspondential to the bones."[70] There is no life or use in the bones without the Spirit of God who inspires us to express truth wisely.

Spiritual Causes and Antidotes for Broken and/or Decayed Teeth

When we are not expressing the truth wisely, we will have problems with our teeth. When we are unreliable to God in a time of need, the scriptures say that we are like a broken tooth:

> "Confidence in an unfaithful man
> in time of trouble is like a broken tooth,
> and a foot out of joint."[71]

When our teeth are broken, it conveys an unstable lifestyle in expressing wisdom in times of need. This can also mean we are negligent in confessing faults or speaking up for what is true and good.

When we have an issue with grinding teeth, we are overstressed and have been vocalizing feelings of anger. Taking a step back from anxiety helps us to re-evaluate our expressions and learn how to better vocalize what is true and good. This will help restore healing energies to the mouth and teeth.

Spiritual Causes and Antidotes for Heartburn

Heartburn causes a burning sensation in the throat area. There are many natural causes. For example, eating spicy or acidic foods or dark chocolate, drinking caffeinated or carbonated drinks, and lying down after eating.

In my personal study, I have found that the spiritual cause for heartburn is saying things that are not true because of anger or pride. The bitterness in our words manifests as bitterness in our throats. We do this when we find fault and voice angry responses.

I experienced heartburn many times, but once in a way that I never had before. It lasted a couple of days and was so pronounced that I ended up in the emergency room, thinking that something was very wrong. After waiting for hours, they prescribed a costly medication that I never ended up getting because of its expense. After my nutritionist informed me that the prescription was not beneficial for the body, I took a look at what I was doing wrong, which I should have done in the beginning.

After thinking about it, it dawned on me how bitter I had been in voicing my own opinions. I realized that I had been saying things that were not true because of anger and pride. Stress was getting the better of me, and the bitterness of my own words was manifesting in my throat. It made so much sense to me.

As soon as I realized it, I prayed over myself to cast out the pride with its bitterness and false accusations. I was shocked to see the resulting effects of the heartburn begin to leave: free of charge. The Lord also showed me to change my eating habits, which had been motivated by anxiety eating. These habits had caused me to be drawn to foods and drinks that increased stomach acid. I am so thankful for Doctor God, working His best in and through human beings.

Keep the Sabbath Day Holy
Nervous System
Good Memory, Calm, and Mediating

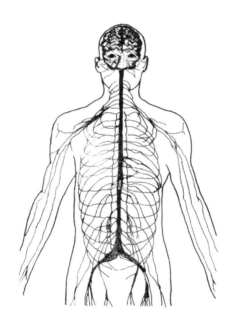

The Fourth Commandment
Figure 7

Chapter 6

The Fourth Commandment

"Remember the sabbath day, to keep it holy.
Six days shalt thou labour, and do all thy work:
but the seventh day is the sabbath of the LORD thy God:
in it thou shalt not do any work,
thou, nor thy son, nor thy daughter,
thy manservant, nor thy maidservant, nor thy cattle,
nor thy stranger that is within thy gates:
for in six days the LORD made heaven and earth,
the sea, and all that in them is, and rested the seventh day:
wherefore the LORD blessed the sabbath day,
and hallowed it."
Exodus 20:8–11; Deuteronomy 5:12–15

After God completed His work of creation, He reflected on all that He did and rested. God blessed this day and set it apart from other days as one of rest and spiritual rejuvenation, a day to reflect on our works and come closer to Him. This day of rest included everyone in the family: housekeepers, servants, guests, and animals. There is a blessing on this day when we take time to hear His voice, study His Word, and introspect on how to become more like Him. This brings healing and refreshment to our spirit, enabling us to live more in tune with Him in our daily lives.

Jesus said that the Sabbath was made for man and not man for the Sabbath. This meant doing good with the gifts and talents that have been given at any time. Jesus set the record straight when He healed on the Sabbath day, despite what the religious authorities thought about it. He also justified His disciples when they plucked corn on the Sabbath because they needed to eat, contrary to the Jewish law of not doing any work on the Sabbath.

Every day to them was the Sabbath because they followed the intent of this commandment: doing God's will for the spiritual and natural care of humanity. This angered the Pharisees, who relied on their literal understanding of this commandment, claiming that Jesus had broken it. They were unable to accept the spiritual application of this law because of their false understanding of it and their love of control.

We live in a very stressful period of time. Family pressures, work demands, financial instability, personal tragedies, environmental dangers, and terrorist threats—all provide us with a sense of unrest. It is a time of testing and reaping as we enter a difficult period of history, learning how to multitask as we manage our coping skills. The up-step in technology and the constant stream of information affects us, and the demands of life keep us on the go. This is a time that was prophesied in Daniel, where it says, "Many shall run to and fro, and knowledge shall be increased."[72] With life as busy as it is, there is little time for God, unless we make it. If we neglect our natural and spiritual needs, we become physically and spiritually exhausted. We remain in a restless state of mind, and our coping skills fail us. The increased anxiety levels slowly begin to overload us, disrupting our nervous system and affecting our natural and spiritual health.

Things being the way they are, there is a great need for rest: rest for our body and, more importantly, rest for our spirit. This kind of rest can only come from God and His Word because it gives us strength and refreshment. It provides us with a spiritual perspective so that we can remain in a peaceful state, knowing God is in control, and remain unaffected by the stress of daily living. Jesus reminds us in Matthew:

"Come unto me, all ye that labour and are heavy laden,
and I will give you rest.
Take my yoke upon you, and learn of me;
for I am meek and lowly in heart:
and ye shall find rest unto your souls.
For my yoke is easy, and my burden is light."[73]

Jesus's words lift the burdens that we place upon ourselves. They provide us with a way of coping that we would not otherwise have. Seeing things from a spiritual perspective lightens our burdens and fills us with a sense of peace that comes from knowing God. When our well is full, we are more ready to be useful to help others in creative ways.

The scriptures teach us that meeting God's need in others is the answer for a speedy recovery from health issues. When we do this, God's life acts as a battery charger for us. We see how this takes place in the book of Isaiah:

> "Is not this the fast that I have chosen?
> to loose the bands of wickedness,
> to undo the heavy burdens,
> and to let the oppressed go free,
> and that ye break every yoke?
> Is it not to deal thy bread to the hungry,
> and that thou bring the poor that are cast out to thy house?
> when thou seest the naked, that thou cover him,
> and that thou hide not thyself from thine own flesh?
> Then shall thy light break forth as the morning,
> and thine health shall spring forth speedily."[74]

It is not only the natural needs here that God is looking for us to fulfill, but the spiritual needs in the lives of others. These needs require wisdom and love to lift heavy burdens in order to free a soul. Give of what you have when you see a need.

> "I shall pass through this world but once.
> Any good therefore that I can do
> or any kindness that I can show
> to any human being,
> let me do it now.
> Let me not defer or neglect it,
> for I shall not pass this way again."[75]

There is a promise of rest that God is offering in the book of Hebrews. As with most promises, it takes personal effort on our part to make it our own.

"Let us therefore fear, lest, a promise being left us
of entering into his rest,
any of you should seem to come short of it.
For unto us was the gospel preached,
as well as unto them:
but the word preached did not profit them,
not being mixed with faith in them that heard it....
For he that is entered into his rest,
he also hath ceased from his own works,
as God did from his.
Let us labour therefore to enter into that rest,
lest any man fall after the same example of unbelief."[76]

There is a warning here that we could possibly miss the rest that God is offering, if we refuse to cease from our own works. This can happen when we do not believe the truth enough to allow it to discipline our actions and enter into a God-given use for others. If we want to do things our own way, without finding out what God thinks about it, we cannot receive a life of peace that comes from knowing Him.

Jesus said that "whosoever will save his life shall lose it: but whosoever will lose his life for my sake, the same shall save it."[77] When we preserve our selfish life, we defend its reactions and dramas. It maintains its life by blaming others and retaliating. The more we defend it, the stronger it gets. We are unable to identify it as our enemy, because we don't know how to let go and move on.

Exercising nonresistance causes us to accept our circumstances without fighting them. In this state, we are only a witness to life's events, without reacting to them. Jesus tried to get this idea across when he told us to turn the other cheek in Matthew 5:39. We feel the sting but manage our reaction by offering the other cheek. In this way, we are not controlled by anger. This takes practice. Having a mind-set of nonresistance tempers our responses to life's hardships. Keeping a stiff upper lip helps to change our human nature into a divine one. Living the words that Jesus taught allows us to remain in our highest energy state. Letting go of negative reactions to life's events brings a little heaven on earth and protects us from the illnesses it causes.

The Nervous System

According to *The Human Body Book*, the central nervous system is composed of the brain and the chief nerve, the spinal cord, which runs along the inside of the spinal column. This network is described as "constantly alive with electricity … so vast and complex that … all the individual nerves from one body joined end to end, could reach around the world two and a half times."[78] Imagine that! Our whole inner world is over twice the circumference of planet earth.

The job of the central nervous system is the coordinator and decision-maker of the body's functions. Twelve pairs of nerves branch from the brain, and thirty-one pairs branch from the cord. As the nerve cells branch out, they send information and receive instructions from the brain and work in the divine order for which they were created. It is no small coincidence that Jesus chose twelve apostles, for each pair of these twelve represents coordinators and decision-makers of the mind and heart of God to best help the body of His chosen people.

When our mind is in alignment with God in thought and deed, there is an increased flow of energy to the brain and spinal cord. When we maintain this state, messages flow through the nerves with the greatest amount of power. This directly influences the health of our nervous system.

Having God's mind operating within us provides our spirit with a sabbath, for when we are doing God's will, we are resting from our own works and enveloped by peace. How well we remain in it will determine the health of this system. When the thoughts and messages we receive from God are put to use through our personality and gifts, the greatest energy and power flows into our nervous system. This provides us with inner peace and satisfaction.

Calmness and Mediation

The two qualities that allow our nervous system to work most effectively are calmness and mediation. When we are calm, we are free from anxiety so that we can think clearly and make proper decisions. Mediation is the act of reconciling differences. This quality diffuses frustration between people so that they can see clearly in order to make the right decisions. Because a large percentage of medical problems are anxiety-based, it is important to operate with a clear mind and a calm attitude to resolve day-to-day issues.

It is God's desire that we master our human nature, especially when it is at its worst. For it is in those situations, when God seems distant, that He wants us to draw from the inner wisdom within us so that we can maintain a good attitude under pressure and develop His nature. Understanding the purpose of those situations helps us accept them as we go through it. This is the first step to mastery. This way, we bring a little more heaven on earth and are able to influence those around us in a positive way. But in order to do this, our self-life nature has to die.

Nervous System Disorders

There are many disorders that affect the nervous system: insomnia, restless leg syndrome, Alzheimer's disease, Parkinson's disease, and others. Because the subject is so vast, we will only be covering these disorders in this book.

Insomnia

The inability to relax and sleep is a great problem today. Pushing ourselves harder than we should and harboring anxiety about situations that we can't control are some of the culprits that keep our nervous system in overdrive. Anxiety that overloads our mind creates an imbalance in our nervous system that affects our sleep rhythms. When it is time to rest, we lose the ability to succumb to the rhythmic embrace of sleep.

Spiritual Causes of Insomnia

Sleep rhythms have a synchronized ebb and flow, just like the tides. When we fight the flow of life's currents by being headstrong, the state of anxiety (fight or flight) can alter this ebb and flow and keep us on, when we should be off, and awake when we should be asleep.

Anxiety reflects a tendency to be overcontrolling. Standards are held too high for ourselves or others. Our patience wears thin as we hold onto these standards and expectations. The anxiety penetrates our spirit and begins controlling us through our own sleep rhythms to show us to ourselves. At some point in life, the build-up of anxiety from the standards that we have held has thrown us emotionally over the edge. Fears have a way of doing this. If we fear being controlled, we draw the controlling fear to us until we get to a point where we can look it in the face, talk to it, and find out why it is there. It may have been buried since childhood, instilled by controlling parents or heredity that has unknowingly become our own.

God allows disruptions in our nervous system to surface, so we can uncover the secret of its control. By getting a good look at how it works and the emotional imbalances that it causes, we can disrupt its methods from having control over us. Once we know what we're doing that is causing it to remain with us by how we're thinking, feeling, or imagining, we will be able to let it go and move on into a greater usefulness. The symptoms producing excessive control of our mind during the sleep cycle have to leave.

Antidotes for Insomnia

> "But let patience have her perfect work, that ye may be perfect and entire, wanting nothing."[79]

Letting go of our expectations helps us maintain an inner peace.

Finding the good in every situation, and knowing God is in control, helps balance stress levels.

> "Except the LORD build the house, they labour in vain that build it … for so he giveth his beloved sleep."[80]

> "So don't be anxious about tomorrow. God will take care of your tomorrow too. Live one day at a time."[81]

Welcome sleep and rest. We need it to provide us with a better perspective and refreshment of spirit and healing on a cellular level.

Dreams and Visions

In some cases, God can only get through to us when we are sleeping, in a coma, or under anesthesia. He waits until we are asleep to use dreams and visions to withdraw us from our present course. Because our pride has made it difficult for Him to talk with us while we are awake, He resorts to the next best possible way, which is while we are sleeping.

It says in Job, "For God speaketh once, yea twice, yet man perceiveth it not. In a dream, in a vision of the night, when deep sleep falleth upon men, in slumberings upon the bed; then he openeth the ears of men, and sealeth their instruction, that he may withdraw man from his purpose, and hide pride from man."[82]

It is only in times of quietness that God can reach our spirit. His wisdom is revealed only when we are quiet and ready to listen.

Spiritual Causes of Restless Leg Syndrome

Restless leg syndrome occurs when overactive nerves produce involuntary twitching or jerking in the legs, especially at night. Because the legs are what we walk with, they represent our "walk" or the application of the truth in our lives. If we are spinning our mental wheels without an application to move forward, the nerves in our legs become restless. It is as if the legs want to go, but anxiety is preventing us from implementing action. A plan is what is needed. This way, the energies will not stagnate in our mind, leaving us without proper footing in our application. Take the necessary steps to put good thoughts into action.

Antidotes for Restless Leg Syndrome

"Ponder the path of thy feet, and let all thy ways be established. Turn not to the right hand nor to the left: remove thy foot from evil."[83]

"Where is the good way, and walk therein, and ye shall find rest for your souls."[84]

"Every place that the sole of your foot shall tread upon, that have I given unto you.... Only be thou strong and very courageous, that thou mayest observe to do according to all the law ... turn not from it to the right hand or to the left, that thou mayest prosper whithersover thou goest."[85]

"He hath shewed thee, O man, what is good; and what doth the LORD require of thee, but to do justly, and to love mercy, and to walk humbly with thy God?"[86]

Memory and Aging

Remembering what is important to God and applying it in life assists in maintaining a good memory. Receiving and applying God's thoughts enhances the flow of energy to our brains and nerve centers. The Spirit of God will always bring to our remembrance principles from the Word of God giving us guidance and direction.

As we age and our body begins to slow down, we may begin to notice memory issues. It is a time of learning how to live more simply. We start off as children, living in the moment and finding delight in the simple things of life. When we are older, the beauty of living in the moment returns to us. We can share with others the wisdom and experience that we have gained throughout the years. This phase of life holds within it times of reflection that help us appreciate the value and purpose of our lives. By looking for more ways to do good, the more new opportunities will find us and open new doors for us to share with others. Documenting our life's journey with friends or family helps us to remember the important milestones in our lives. What we have learned and experienced will someday help another, in this world and in the world to come. Always be appreciative for your life and the experiences you have gained. It was lived for a divine purpose and has made you the person you are today. Embrace the mellowing of aging.

Alzheimer's Disease

Alzheimer's disease, which is a form of dementia, is caused by an abnormal production of a protein in the brain. This causes people to lose their memories. This blockage of protein represents a block in dealing with the real issues in life. As a result, we are kept from remembering what is truly important in our own lives.

Spiritual Causes of Alzheimer's Disease

Alzheimer's disease corresponds to forgetting God in our lives. The disease reveals its own cause. According to *God Can Heal You,* Alzheimer's reflects a "refusal to use knowledges learned (in memory) for God and good; laziness in applying God's Word to life's situations."[87] When we forget God's reality and do not maintain the truths that we know by applying them in life, we will find ourselves incapable of remembering what is important in our own lives.

Antidotes for Alzheimer's Disease

"Let thine heart retain my words: keep my commandments, and live. Get wisdom, get understanding: forget it not; neither decline from the words of my mouth. Forsake her not, and she shall preserve thee: love her, and she shall keep thee."[88]

"But whoso looketh into the perfect law of liberty, and continueth therein, he being not a forgetful hearer, but a doer of the work, this man shall be blessed in his deed."[89]

"Beware that thou forget not the LORD thy God, in not keeping his commandments, and his judgments, and his statutes, which I command thee this day... and thou say in thine heart, My power and the might of mine hand hath gotten me this wealth. But thou shalt remember the LORD thy God: for it is he that giveth thee power to get wealth … And it shall be, if thou do at all forget the LORD thy God … ye shall surely perish."[90]

"But the Comforter, which is the Holy Ghost, whom the Father will send in my name, he shall teach you all things, and bring all things to your remembrance, whatsoever I have said unto you."[91]

Parkinson's Disease

Parkinson's is a neurological disorder in the brain. According to *The Human Body,* "The disease causes weakness and stiffness of the muscles and interferes with speech, walking, and performance of daily tasks…. There is often a tremor of the person's hands when they are at rest."[92] Parkinson's is caused by a chemical imbalance in the brain, which is short of the required amount of dopamine, a neurotransmitter. Dopamine is a substance that allows nerve cells to communicate with each other. *The Human Body* also says, "In a normal brain, the levels of dopamine and acetylcholine are evenly balanced. In Parkinson's disease the levels of dopamine are reduced and acetylcholine is relatively overactive."[93] These two transmitters must work together to control the body's balance to produce the stability for a normal, operative state for the muscles to move. A healthy brain requires proper communication from these messengers in the cells so that the rest of the body is able to function in its highest, most useful state. If the mind does not properly communicate to the rest of the body, the muscles become limited and restricted.

Spiritual Causes of Parkinson's Disease

According to *God Can Heal You,* this disease is caused by "stubborn refusal to trust in God; refusal to look to God in time of trouble; fearfulness in trusting God; public-opinion minded."[94]

When we have other loves that we trust in other than God, it is very easy to lose control during a troublous time. We can lose hope and focus more on protecting ourselves. When life consists of feeling abandoned, losing hope, and running away from fearful situations, we become spiritually immobile and paralyzed by situations and people who produce it. We leave off communicating with God who could walk us through these fears. When this mind-set is held for years without resolution, the effects begin to reflect themselves in the body. The habitual fear and stress create a deficiency of dopamine and an overproduction of acetylcholine to the nerve cells. This condition is created either from our own lifestyle or the behavioral weaknesses inherited through the genes of our ancestors. The cells become so inundated that they can no longer communicate proper nerve signals to the muscles, and they begin to lose their functionality.

In the book *You Can Heal Your Life,* fear and control are the producing causes of Parkinson's disease.[95] Fear causes one to be overcontrolling. Heightened, prolonged fear hinders the production and balance of neurotransmitters from reaching the cells which would keep them functioning correctly.

In the book *A More Excellent Way to Be in Health,* some of the spiritual causes of Parkinson's disease are "unresolved rejection, massive amounts of abandonment, rejection and hope deferred."[96] Abandonment from a spouse or children can leave a person with heightened fear and anxiety. There are many causes of abandonment: neglect, abuse, divorce, or death. When our hopes and expectations are cut off, the prolonged stress affects the production of our neurotransmitters. The mind causes the body to reflect its emotional state; it loses its control and slips into a state of imbalance and unrest.

Antidotes for Parkinson's Disease

The development of love and trust in God as having control over life is vital for healing this disease. Facing our fears and resolving situations within ourselves can bring us a renewed trust in the goodness of God. This involves letting go of past situations that have produced these fears. This, in turn, will diminish the effects of being overcontrolling, which usually masks our worst fears. Approaching how we feel internally with a calm, introspective attitude can give us the faith we need to identify them in our lives.

God within us can walk us through these fears by inspiring us to write down the thoughts and feelings that we have held in for so long. Different people have different ways of resolving fears. A friend of mine with Parkinson's had her catharsis by taking a pen and writing down her feelings on pieces of paper, a little each day. We made continual trips for a few weeks to visit a quiet, peaceful spot by a lake, a park that reminded her of a place she had once loved. When she finished her writing, she burned the papers in a pan over an outside fire pit. Then we scattered the ashes to the wind. For her, this gesture was a way to let go of the negative effects that life's hurts had on her. This way, she could let go and move on with resolve.

Creating a new perspective from our deferred hope sometimes needs a symbolic gesture. This is a confirmation of our commitment to move forward. It strengthens our faith in God's plan, which many times we cannot perceive under duress. This faith gives us hope. We may not see its results in the present, but it plants an eternal seed that springs forth within us. Faith and hope provide strength to a wounded spirit. However, hope that is seen is not hope. Whatever illness has plagued us in this world, if we have done our best to deal with its spiritual causes, God will assist in its resolve in the next life. Our resolving of issues provides us with a foundation that enables us to move forward and progress in life's journey.

> "Surely I have behaved and quieted myself, as a child that is weaned of his mother: my soul is even as a weaned child."[97]

> "Commit thy works unto the LORD, and thy thoughts shall be established."[98]

Trust increases our dependency upon God and fills us with an inward satisfaction of knowing who we are, despite our outward circumstances.

The following poem came to me during a time of great duress, providing me with spiritual insight:

The Journey

Can I in the storm of my heredity be still
when the rage of false emotions
claiming to be right
threaten the fiber of my nerve and sinew?

Can I withdraw from their clamor and
walk upon the stillness of the waves
of reality and truth?
Can I look fear in the face and remain unafraid
only to discover love's cloak and
remain un-fooled by her appearance?
Can I look beyond the natural world
to strive with my being,
to glimpse the reality of the world that awaits,
knowing my true friends dwell in the world beyond?
I cannot but long to be home where neither
pain, nor strife, nor hate, nor vice
impersonate the loving God that I was born to know.
Alas, I wait for journey's end to lead me home
where appearances cannot lie
and truth embodies creative life
and love transforms my very soul.
I find a new creature there whose emotions carry no fear,
harbor no grudge, but bear the fruit of understanding
of how to live life without reacting to it
knowing the eternal plan is woven in it
for my ultimate good.
Bound by willing entry, I learn and live,
understanding that life is not what it appears to be.
It stands as a cycle, a mere season and shadow
of what will be—ever moving on
as its message unfolds and reveals its purpose.
Indeed, we partner with God,
spinning a cloak that becomes the
fiber of our eternal being,
bringing us into the reality of the life within
that knows no bounds.
We stand alone as the creator of our eternal fate.

Honor Thy Father
and Thy Mother
Muscles, Ligaments, and Sinew
Obedience

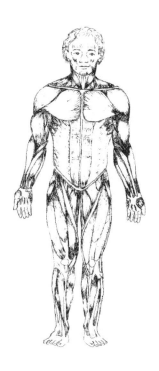

The Fifth Commandment
Figure 8

Chapter 7

The Fifth Commandment

"Honor thy father and thy mother: that thy days may be long
upon the land which the LORD thy God giveth thee."
Exodus 20:12; Deuteronomy 5:16

Honoring our parents allows us to have a long and healthy life. When we obey our parents to do what is right, we are honoring God, for they are God's image and likeness as a man and woman. Respecting those who God has placed over us for our good acknowledges the goodness and truth that they helped instill in us as children.

The scriptures refer to God as a mother, father, husband, and a wife. In the book of Isaiah, God relates His feelings as a mother toward Israel when He says, "Can a woman forget her sucking child, that she should not have compassion on the son of her womb? yea, they may forget, yet will I not forget thee."[99] Every mother knows her feelings toward her children, and God has these feelings in a more divine and eternal way than we can ever know. We should never doubt the love God has for us. As a mother and a father, God takes serious interest in the welfare of His children.

Single-Parent Families

Children more than ever need to know that God is their true Father and Mother. Sadly, half of all families today are single-parent families. This may be due to divorce, drug or alcohol abuse, or death. God has a special place in His heart for those who live without the loving support of a mother and father. He watches over them daily and stands in their defense to provide for their needs.

In the Psalms, God is referred to as "a father of the fatherless."[100] In conditions where a father or mother is not present, God steps in as the spiritual caregiver and inspires direction in ways unknown to us to protect and help them. God's presence is a comfort and a very present help to them in times of need.

"When my father and my mother forsake me,
then the LORD will take me up."[101]

Jesus Being Fatherless

Jesus was naturally fatherless because He had no natural, biological father. Jesus was conceived by the Word of God through the angel Gabriel. God truly was His Father, who He obeyed and spoke to throughout His life. Jesus honored Him by expressing the inspirations that came to Him through the scriptures. He reminded us to follow His example when He said, "Call no man your father upon the earth: for one is your Father, which is in heaven."[102] Jesus honored God first because He is the one, true Father who gives life to us all. Jesus fashioned His life to become one with Him in everything that He said and did through His application of the Word and the Spirit of God.

How We View Our Parents

The way we have treated our parents reflects how we feel about God as a man and a woman. Parents are the first ones we have a relationship with as a child, for they are in God's stead when we are young. We formulate our understanding of right and wrong as well as our relationships from their influence. If we had a bad relationship with them, we need to look within to help us understand how we may be superimposing this view on the way we see and understand God. It may or may not be true about how God really is, but it may have become our truth. It is very thought provoking and needs our introspection.

If we have long-standing grudges toward our parents, we need to resolve them, for this affects our health and longevity. If we hold onto grudges, we end up emulating the negative qualities our parents had, without even being aware. Resolving these past hurts and wounds helps us heal and elevates our mind to see the good that they did in whatever capacity they were capable of. With this new perspective, we can let go of the past negative spiral without disliking our parents or ourselves. Whatever situations God has allowed is to help us develop into a stronger person for our eternal betterment.

It is all how we look at it. Finding the good lessons in life from our relationship with our parents is very freeing for our spirit. The more thankful we are for the situations we experienced, whether good or bad, the freer and healthier we become. By embracing positive thoughts of love and understanding, negative thoughts and feelings have to go.

Jesus's Obedience to His Leadings as a Child

Jesus's depth of understanding brought new meaning to the commandment of honoring our parents, for He was true to the leadings of the Spirit of wisdom in His life. He knew when it was best to obey God's impressions before the wishes of His parents. He followed these leadings at an early age. When He was twelve, He was asked by His parents, who had been looking for Him for three days, where He was after they had left the Passover celebration. They thought He was with the family. When they realized He wasn't with them, they went to look for him and found Him in the temple. He answered them and said that He had to be about His Father's business. After He had finished speaking to the religious leaders, He submitted to His parents and headed home with them. Jesus followed His inspiration to talk with religious leaders at the early age of twelve, even at the expense of being left behind. Jesus knew that there were times when following God was more important than going along with His family's wishes. He did this not to be rebellious but to grab a moment of opportunity, in order to follow the inspiration that God put on His heart.

It is not often revealed to others what the will of God is for us individually. It is a personal journey that requires individual faith, many times to the disliking of our family and friends.

Jesus gave clarity to what it means to honor our parents when He said, "Who is my mother, or my brethren?... For whosoever shall do the will of God, the same is my brother, and my sister, and mother."[103] Jesus chose to define His family as those who did God's will. Doing God's will always took precedence over what His mother, father, brothers, or sisters wanted. The bond of loyalty was first to those who desired God's will, and family came second. Obeying and doing God's will is what defines and bonds a true family in the mind of God.

Jesus followed His Father's leadings through the end of His life, laying aside His own understanding and the power He had to free Himself from His own death. He trusted His Father to the end, even though the prospects of deliverance looked dim. This is true obedience of a Son to a Father. As conveyed in Hebrews, "Though he were a Son, yet learned he obedience by the things which he suffered."[104] Life took its course, and He accepted the path that He had to follow. His pattern of obedience established an eternal link with the Spirit of God within Him that could never be taken from Him. He did this by capturing every thought and bringing it into the obedience of His Father's will. This is the example that He left for us.

The Spirit of obedience and overcoming is what Jesus has offered to those who love Him enough to discipline their life as He did. Keeping the commandments the way that He taught them develops a divine nature within our personality. This qualifies us and allows us to become candidates for true sonship. As it says in Romans, "For as many as are led by the Spirit of God, they are the sons of God."[105]

We are reminded about the health benefits of being led by God in the Living Bible translation in Proverbs:

> "If you want a long and satisfying life,
> closely follow my instructions.
> Never tire of loyalty and kindness.
> Hold these virtues tightly.
> Write them deep within your heart.
> If you want favor with both God and man,
> and a reputation for good judgment and common
> sense, then trust the Lord completely;
> don't ever trust yourself.

In everything you do, put God first, and he will direct
you and crown your efforts with success.
Don't be conceited, sure of your own wisdom.
Instead, trust and reverence the Lord,
and turn your back on evil; when you do that,
then you will be given renewed health and vitality."[106]

Obedience: The Health of the Muscles

Just as water, oxygen, and movement are the key to having healthy muscles, so also is obedience to the Spirit of God. Obedience allows us to be stretched and made pliable for our greatest use. It keeps our mind flexible to the ever-moving Spirit. The scriptures teach that the Spirit is given to those who obey. Obedience to God's leadings is the key to energizing the blood flow through the muscles, ligaments, and tendons. The degree of our flexibility to God's thoughts and leadings are reflected in the condition of our muscles.

When we follow these leadings against our own will, we free ourselves from stubbornness that restricts the energy flow to the muscles. Our job is to feel after God and find Him, just as a son or daughter would seek advice from a good parent. Making right choices to obey God's leadings not only helps to heal the muscles, it perfects our character and qualifies us for entrance into a heavenly life. God urges us to make the right decisions for our own health's sake in the scripture below:

"Look, today I have set before you life and death,
depending on whether you obey or disobey....
Oh, that you would choose life;
that you and your children might live!
Choose to love the Lord your God
and to obey him and to cling to him,
for he is your life
and the length of your days."[107]

Following God's impressions means that we are open to obeying our first thoughts and first feelings. These are usually the most accurate and carry with them God's initial inspiration. It is much easier to hear them when we are quiet or alone. For me, that is either early in the morning or in the quiet of the night. Thoughts are clearer and insightful. The more we follow these quiet thoughts and inspirations, the more sensitive and freer we become.

Following God's leadings will always keep your energy levels high. For example, God will always inspire you to leave an event in the bloom. When the need is met wherever you are, the energy will begin to wane slightly. That is the best time to go. Otherwise, if you delay past the time, your energy begins to deplete. Being aware of your energy levels requires awareness and flexibility. Notice which people or events elevate your energy and which ones deplete it. These are telltale signs to follow. God's Spirit is always energizing and recharges your battery. Be flexible at a moment's notice to make a change in your plans when the urge and the signs are there to do so. Your energy will then heighten as you follow them.

Spiritual Causes of Muscle Problems

Muscle problems reveal the inability to listen to God's instruction and adapt to change. Extending our will too far and for too long can cause us to experience muscle problems. Inflexibility in our mind-set can also cause our muscles to become restricted, knotted, or torn, restricting our movability. The muscles contract and envelope us as a tightening "web," as one physical therapist put it. These muscles remain in this restricted state until they are rehabilitated and stretched back out through physical therapy. When we have made a habit of saying no to God in some area of our life because we are set in our ways, our body follows suit and begins to reflect our restricted thought patterns. When this happens, our muscles begin to speak to us through strains, tears, arthritis, or rheumatism. Our attitude is what has restricted us from going any further. What is it that drives us this way? A preconceived idea, a standard we are holding onto, or just plain stubbornness.

Spiritual Causes of Carpal Tunnel, Knee, and Shoulder Problems

Where the muscle problems are in the body will give us a clue as to their spiritual cause. If they are in the hand, such as carpal tunnel syndrome, there is a problem with being strong-willed and inflexible in the way that we work. This is because the hand corresponds to our works. If muscle problems are affecting our knees, there is a problem with humility. Problems with the knees generally reflect a pride that is unwilling to submit to God's progressive leadings. This is because of previous standards that we are holding onto. The knees allow us to lower ourselves, which reflect a humble and flexible state of mind. The knees also represent prayer, for we talk with God with bended knees and submit ourselves to His control. If muscle problems are affecting our shoulders, we are imposing false burdens upon ourselves. Our past understanding of what God wants and how things should be has become our present burden.

By re-evaluating our understanding to see things in a higher light, we can identify what is blocking us and see things in a progressive light. In this way, we lift the burdens we have placed upon ourselves so that we bring greater happiness and usefulness into our life.

Religious Duty, Habit, and Repetition

Religious duty and habit are rigid standard-makers. There is a place for duty, but not when it restricts God in our lives. Jesus tried to free us from the idea of religious duty in Matthew when He said, "Don't recite the same prayer over and over as the heathen do, who think prayers are answered only by repeating them again and again. Remember, your Father knows exactly what you need even before you ask him!"[108] God would rather us talk to Him with heartfelt honesty than limit Him to repetitious prayer or ceremonial worship on Sunday. Religious duty can be a clever way of separating us from our much-needed personal time with God.

Talking with God

In the movie *Joan of Arc*, one of Joan's pleas to the religious ministers who were persecuting her was that she felt they were punishing her for talking to God. God had given her answers to present-day problems. Her willingness to implement them caused her to act outside the box of standardized religion. Her inspiration and love for God gave her an avenue for personal expression and direction in her life.

I believe that everyone who truly knows God for themselves, or wants to, will be misunderstood in their journey with God, especially by those in religious authority. People with great minds and spiritual insight are often rejected by those in authority blinded by power, prejudice, or established standards. It is the tendency in humans to follow the group who yells the loudest or has the most power. This causes you to lose control and blind you from better judgment. Lost in the mob mentality, they cannot think or see that they are persecuting a righteous or innocent person. This has happened throughout our history with examples such as Jesus, Gandhi, and Martin Luther King. They used their God-given intelligence to courageously oppose what was considered highly popular and accepted as normal thinking.

I believe this intelligence is given to each of us through God-given gifts to help solve present and future problems that mankind is presently facing. God wants to work through individuals who know Him personally to make this world a better place. If what God showed people in every field of life was implemented, we could prevent future problems from occurring on this planet. I encourage you to find your individual voice and develop the talents that God has given you.

We are living in a time of great, impending trouble. By charting your own course, you can begin to find your purpose for being here. As the objective becomes clearer, the gifts and talents that have lain dormant within you will become activated, bringing you into alignment with the need that God shows you. Assisting others will enable you to draw on the miraculous so that you can, as Jesus did, not only multiply loaves and fishes, but be a vehicle for healing, guidance, and direction.

The following principles will help free us from muscle problems and make us more sensitive and pliable to God:

Antidotes for Muscle Problems

Do not let the initial reaction of being shown your weaknesses prevent you from changing your behavior. Minimize the hurt by seeing the good that it is doing to make you a stronger person, preparing you for your future.

"A wise man will hear, and will increase learning; and a man of understanding shall attain unto wise counsels.... The fear of the LORD is the beginning of knowledge: but fools despise wisdom and instruction. My son, hear the instruction of thy father, and forsake not the law of thy mother: for they shall be an ornament of grace unto thy head, and chains about thy neck."[109]

It is better to get the lesson the first time, so you do not have to experience the situation again. Grab your moment of opportunity and learn from it, for it is allowed by God to develop a certain quality in you that you will need in the future.

"My son, despise not the chastening of the LORD; neither be weary of his correction: for whom the LORD loveth he correcteth; even as a father the son in whom he delighteth."[110]

There is an eternal good designed in every hardship.

"Children, obey your parents; this is the right thing to do because God has placed them in authority over you. Honor your father and mother. This is the first of God's Ten Commandments that ends with a promise. And this is the promise ... that if you honor your father and mother, yours will be a long life, full of blessing. And now a word to you parents. Don't keep on scolding and nagging your children, making them angry and resentful. Rather, bring them up with the loving discipline the Lord himself approves, with suggestions and godly advice."[111]

"Obey them that have the rule over you, and submit yourselves: for they watch for your souls, as they that must give account."[112]

Spiritual Correspondences of the Neck and Stiff-Neckedness

The neck corresponds to our free will in obeying the truth. It is the connection between our mind and heart. When our neck muscles become stiff or injured, it reflects an attitude of being self-willed. We are deliberately refusing to cooperate with God on some point. Below are some scriptures that lend some clarity on the spiritual meaning:

> "I knew that thou art obstinate, and thy neck is an iron sinew, and thy brow brass."[113]

> "But they obeyed not, neither inclined their ear, but made their neck stiff, that they might not hear, nor receive instruction."[114]

> "For I know thy rebellion, and thy stiff neck ... ye have been rebellious against the LORD."[115]

Antidotes for a Stiff Neck

> "What does the Lord your God require of you except to listen carefully to all he says to you, and to obey for your own good the commandments I am giving you today, and to love him, and to worship him with all your hearts and souls?"[116]

> "Therefore, cleanse your sinful hearts and stop your stubbornness."[117]

> "Speak not with a stiff neck."[118]

Your way is not the only standard. Be open to the truth, and learn new ways of doing things better.

> "Turn you at my reproof: behold, I will pour out my spirit unto you, I will make known my words unto you."[119]

Thou Shalt Not Kill
Liver, Gallbladder, Spleen, and Skin
Love, Longsuffering, and Forgiveness

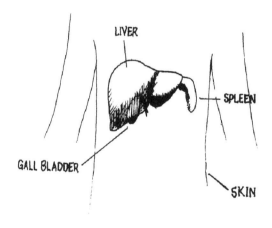

The Sixth Commandment
Figure 9

Chapter 8

The Sixth Commandment

Exodus 20:13; Deuteronomy 5:17
"Thou shalt not kill."

The Lord is the giver of all life. To harm another human being is against His nature.

Cain was the first to murder, killing his brother, Abel, because he was jealous. His brother's sacrifice to God was more acceptable than his. Abel's sacrifice was done with a motive of love, but Cain's was not. As a result, Cain was very angry. God asked him why he was angry and told him that if he did well, he would be accepted. If not, sin would lie at his door (Genesis 4:7). He left the choice up to Cain. When Cain murdered his brother, God asked Him where Abel was. Cain found fault with Him and said, "Am I my brother's keeper?"[120] After Abel's blood cried to God from the ground, He told Cain that he was cursed, and the ground that he tilled would not produce fruit. He would be a vagabond in the earth.

Anger, if not addressed, brings to birth the hurt or destruction of another person, whether by word or deed. We live in a world where hatred and grudges are rampant and are escalating across the board. People are plotting the murder of fellow human beings because of their differences. Increasing terrorism shows hatred intensifying because of different beliefs. School shootings are on the rise because of grudges that are not addressed. Disgruntled employees resent the actions of their coworkers and try to make a wrong right by murdering them. People feel that the color of their skin is superior and kill those who are different.

Sadly, these acts are done at the expense of the life of God in other human beings.

> "When man harms in thought, or word or deed
> another man, he does a wrong to God."[121]

Jesus: On Killing and Anger

Jesus equated killing with anger. In the Living Bible, Jesus said, "Under the laws of Moses the rule was, 'If you murder, you must die.' But I have added to that rule, and tell you that if you are only angry, even in your own home, you are in danger of judgment! If you call your friend an idiot, you are in danger of being brought before the court. And if you curse him, you are in danger of the fires of hell."[122]

Jesus urged us to address unresolved anger in our personal lives so that it does not cause damage to ourselves or others. He taught us to counteract hatred by doing something good for those we hate. This shifts our focus off of our negative emotions and into a good action to counteract its magnetism.

> "Love your enemies, bless them that curse you,
> do good to them that hate you, and pray for them
> which despitefully use you, and persecute you."[123]

When we do not respond by feeding our hatred, it will eventually die and have no power over us. Jesus mastered this on the way to His death, for He responded with love and truth at the height of His anxiety and pain. This is a true Master at work, for He was able to identify His enemy and go to His death as He destroyed it. What an example of a disciplined, overcoming life. This kind of discipline is what destroys hatred and fear, the source of all stress and illness.

> "Hate is a cruel word. If men hate you, regard it not;
> and you can turn the hate of men
> to love and mercy and good will....
> With good destroy the bad;

with generous deeds make avarice ashamed;
with truth make straight
the crooked lines that error draws,
for error is but truth distorted, gone astray.
And pain will follow him
who speaks or acts with evil thoughts....
He is a greater man who conquers self
than he who kills a thousand men in war.
He is the noble man who is himself
what he believes that other men should be.
Return to him who does you wrong your purest love,
and he will cease from doing wrong;
for love will purify the heart of him who is beloved
as truly as it purifies the heart of him who loves."[124]

There are different ways you can prevent anger from taking over in your life. Talking with God about those you do not like can free you from the pent-up frustration of not being heard or understood. Setting time aside to go for a walk or drive can help you gain a new perspective. When you are in a calm state, arrange to talk with the person causing the frustration, if you cannot resolve it alone. Whatever you see in someone else that you do not like is really a part of yourself. Anger would like you to keep your mind so fixated on their faults so that you continue giving your energy to it. Anger has a tendency to blind good judgment. By shifting your focus off of it and taking some time out, you can see things from a clearer perspective. This helps loosen its stronghold on you.

Overcoming evil by doing good is what purifies our spirit. In the book *The Word of the Lord and the Spirit of the Lord,* we learn how to do this: "Find people who hate you and go do something nice for them. Think of that. Think how that would free you. Think how happy you would be.... Love is not a saying, love is a living of the saying.... God gives reward to people who love people who hate them and try to soften their hate and win them down.... I have just taught you ... what perfection in the sight of God is. Doing what you hate. Doing what you don't like. Killing the evil in you and restoring the good in others who have hurt you. And you keep on until it no longer bothers you, and you see God answering your prayer."[125]

Applying Jesus's words teaches us how we can release the disease-producing hatreds that lodge within us. Living the truth disengages evil. If we do not apply the truth, the resentments eat away at us and begin to affect our immune system. The stress of harboring grudges overwhelms the system and begins to render it defenseless. By identifying our hatreds and counteracting them with good actions, we remove their power over us. This can help us stop creating disease within our lives. By utilizing the truth to purge our mind, we deny ourselves the pleasure of responding to our self-life. This is the foundational message contained in Jesus's teachings that keeps our mind and body whole.

Love, Longsuffering, and Forgiveness

A good attitude maintained with love, longsuffering, and forgiveness will allow our body to work in its highest capacity to purge it from toxins. In the following scripture, we will see the application of how we can instill these qualities:

Peter asked Jesus a question: "Lord, how oft shall my brother sin against me, and I forgive him? till seven times? Jesus saith unto him, I say not unto thee, Until seven times: but, Until seventy times seven."[126] This is four hundred and ninety times. Jesus revealed to Peter the limited standards of forgiveness that he was using and emphasized the necessity of remaining in a forgiving state when it comes to people's faults. Making mistakes is a part of life. If we want to be forgiven, we must forgive others (and ourselves) on a continual basis. In order to do this, we must maintain the love of God in our life by bearing the faults of others.

From God's perspective, He would rather we resolve our grudges with our friend, brother, or neighbor first before tithing. This is how much emphasis He places on it. We cannot truly love God without giving up our self-life that longs to dominate and hold grudges.

"Therefore if thou bring thy gift to the altar,
and there rememberest that
thy brother hath aught against thee;
leave there thy gift before the altar,
and go thy way;

first be reconciled to thy brother,
and then come and offer thy gift.
Agree with thine adversary quickly,
whiles thou art in the way with him."[127]

If we want to live with God, we have to act like Him. There is no other way to enter heaven. Instilling these principles makes us like Him. They provide us with a way out of our hereditary nature that is crucial for healing the spirit and body.

Liver, Gallbladder, Spleen, and Skin

The liver, gallbladder, spleen, and skin are the organs that are governed by this commandment, for they are responsible for removing toxins and purifying evils that would harm the body. We can see the location of these organs in Figure 9.

Resentment and Its Effects

When deep-seated resentments are held within over long periods of time, they become a part of our belief system, which our mind begins to call good. Our body begins to produce the fruit of these thoughts, because they have not been separated from our lives. The internal stress that this places on the liver, gallbladder, spleen, and skin weakens their capacity to purge the body. As a result, liver diseases, cancers, gallstones, and problems with the spleen and skin appear.

Spiritual Correspondences of the Liver

The liver corresponds to interior purification because its job is to purge the blood and make it useful for the body. Spiritually speaking, the liver works to separate resentments and hatreds instilled into our blood from negative thought patterns. We see in the book *Physiological Correspondences* that these resentful thoughts "prevent harmonious cooperation with others, especially such as are self-asserting, bitter, and fault-finding."[128] When these qualities are not addressed in life, the function of the liver is affected, and it becomes sluggish and loses its ability to properly purge the blood.

Our job is to address the attributes of an overcritical mind-set by identifying its patterns in our lives. Once we see them, look at them as a separate entity. Cast them out in Jesus's name and replace them with angels of longsuffering, love, and forgiveness. Begin to work on applying these qualities for the next three weeks, until it becomes a habit. As the negative feelings arise, counteract them with actions of longsuffering and kindness. Doing this on a daily basis will begin to eliminate stress on the liver and undo the habitual reactions that we have previously allowed.

Spiritual Causes for Cirrhosis of the Liver

Cirrhosis of the liver is spiritually caused by harboring hatreds and refusing to address them. Feelings of hatred can be overwhelming and cause us to feel hopeless. Many bury their feelings in excessive alcohol use to escape their inward animosity, eventually damaging the liver. This leads them down the road to the self-destructive lifestyle that is noted in the book of Isaiah:

> "Woe unto them that rise up early in the morning,
> that they may follow strong drink;
> that continue until night, till wine inflame them!"[129]

By facing our hurts and resolving them, we eliminate the stress we have inadvertently placed upon our liver. Resolving pent-up anger restores energy back to the liver so that it can effectively perform its purging work for the body. There must be a willingness to see ourselves from a higher perspective in order to realize the damage that unresolved hatred causes. A desire for truth can give us the uplifting strength to get to the root cause of these feelings. Many times, the walls that we put up seem to be our protection, but they are the very barriers that prevent our own recovery.

Spiritual Causes for Hepatitis

Hepatitis is spiritually caused by harboring intense hatreds that have been solidified within ourselves. As a result, our source of life (blood) becomes contaminated, for we have not addressed them, inadvertently calling them good. The natural result is an inflamed liver caused by a virus from contaminated water, food, or blood. These cause the liver to swell, producing uncleanness in the body. We draw to us circumstances that are reflective of our inward state with God. Below are some antidotes that help provide spiritual direction and healing for liver diseases.

Antidotes for Hepatitis and Liver Diseases

"Wherefore laying aside all malice, and all guile, and hypocrisies, and envies, and all evil speakings, as newborn babes, desire the sincere milk of the word, that ye may grow thereby."[130]

"A wise man restrains his anger and overlooks insults. This is to his credit."[131]

"If we confess our sins, he is faithful and just to forgive us our sins, and to cleanse us from all unrighteousness."[132]

The Gallbladder

The gallbladder is about the size of a small pear and is connected to the liver and the intestines by the bile duct. This is a sac for storing bile, which is the substance the body needs for digesting fats.

The Spiritual Correspondence of the Gallbladder

The job of the gallbladder spiritually is to identify and remove deep-seated hatreds toward the love and goodness of God. Holding onto bitterness within us turns our heart away from what is good and true. The effect produces a build-up of inward toxins, which we will refer to as gall, as we see from the following scripture: "Lest there should be among you man, or woman, or family, or tribe, whose heart turneth away this day from the LORD our God, to go and serve the gods of these nations; lest there should be among you a root that beareth gall and wormwood."[133] Gall is a poisonous plant. "Wormwood" means bitterness in Hebrew. When our hearts turn away from God, bitterness fills it. As a result, we cannot produce the proper fruit in our lives because we have been overcome by the bitterness of poisonous emotions, referred to as "gall." Our gallbladder was created to remove this gall.

Gallstones and the Spiritual Causes

Gallstones are the stones in the gallbladder that correspond to bitter resentments and jealousies that have become lodged in our spirit. They result, naturally speaking, from an abnormal metabolizing of cholesterol in bile salts. These stones then become lodged in the bile duct. These stones are there because resentments and jealousies were left unresolved. They are allowed to surface so that we can see them for what they represent and remove them from our lifestyle. Below are some antidotes to help us address them:

Antidotes for Gallstones

"Repent therefore of this thy wickedness, and pray God, if perhaps the thought of thine heart may be forgiven thee. For I perceive that thou art in the gall of bitterness and in the bond of iniquity."[134]

"Stop being mean, bad-tempered and angry. Quarreling, harsh words, and dislike of others should have no place in your lives. Instead, be kind to each other, tenderhearted, forgiving one another, just as God has forgiven you because you belong to Christ."[135]

"Looking diligently lest any man fail of the grace of God; lest any root of bitterness springing up trouble you, and thereby many be defiled."[136]

"Forgive, and ye shall be forgiven."[137]

"Never criticize or condemn—or it will all come back on you. Go easy on others."[138]

The Spleen

According to the book *The Human Body,* the spleen is "a lymphatic organ on the left side of the abdominal cavity that removes and destroys worn-out, *red blood cells* and helps fight infection."[139] The spleen is the largest organ in the lymphatic system. It fights off foreign invaders that would compromise it. Lymphocytes recognize these invaders, so they can be targeted and destroyed from the body. They are the first responders to infections.

Spiritual Correspondences of the Spleen

Because the spleen destroys worn-out blood cells that are no longer useful, the spiritual job of the spleen is to purge our lives from attachments that we have made to people, things, and ideas that have prevented us from spiritually progressing in life. In doing so, we receive new inspirations for greater use and purpose for God and others in our lives. According to *Physiological Correspondences,* "Any who suffer themselves to be hindered in their usefulness by too strong attachments to persons and ways, or by too limited views or set opinions, need to be brought within the influence of the spleen, that their states of life may be taken out of their routine and thoroughly examined.... Minds in which this work is not well done, which adhere tenaciously to by-gones, and therefore do not come into the pleasant relations with new things that are both true and good, but are disposed to complain of evils which arise simply from their own lack of sympathy and charity, are popularly called 'spleeny.'"[140] These strong attachments dull the mind and rob our inspiration. This results in stagnation of spirit because we have inadvertently leveled off in our usefulness to God and others.

Antidotes for Spleen Problems

For a healthy spleen, we need to re-evaluate our attachments to people, things, and opinions that have prevented us from moving forward in life: attachments that have hindered our originality, individuality, and personal expressions in life. Expanding our limited views and perspectives will allow us greater access to our personal creativity. When we let go of past opinions, people, and attachments that rob our energy, we will find new direction and purpose. Look to answer the need that God places on your heart that will benefit others. Kindling this desire to believe in our personal inspiration will not only give us direction, it will also be an inspiration to others. We can only inspire others to the degree that we are inspired. God's love is activated by continual use. In this way, our well of inspiration is maintained, and we are able to let go and let God direct us in the avenues that will open new doors for us.

Blood Cells and Cancer

Normally, the body's natural functions have an built-in healing system. Blood cells that compose body tissue repair damaged, worn-out cells. The blood cells stop forming then when their healing job is done.

In the *Encyclopedia and Dictionary of Medicine and Nursing,* we learn how cancer cells grow: "In cancer, cell growth is unregulated. The cells continue to reproduce until they form a mass of tissue known as a tumor.... Malignant tumors grow in a disorganized fashion, interrupting body functions and robbing normal cells of their food and blood supply. The malignant cells may spread to other parts of the body."[141] The immune system becomes compromised as these cells rob the life of God from other cells in the body. When the cells are out of divine order, they lose their ability to function within the body.

Spiritual Causes for Cancer

Cancer is spiritually caused from an unidentified rejection of God's love. It remains unidentified because error in some degree has taken on the appearance of truth, and the belief system has become compromised. Habitual reactions of repressed rage have become a person's worst enemy. Inward anger has unknowingly become a standard of right and wrong, leading a person to openly justify grudges and resentments. These emotions inundate the immune system and render it powerless in fighting off cancer. *Type C Connection* says that "bottling up one's feelings can throw the biological switch that turns cells malignant."[142] When we refuse to give love because of how we feel about ourselves, we can find it very easy to accuse another of being unloving. When we cannot forgive, we weaken the immune system.

It is so important to love ourselves enough to examine our feelings in order to resolve the animosities that are present in our life.

"If you are angry, don't sin by nursing your grudge.
Don't let the sun go down with you still angry—
get over it quickly; for when you are angry
you give a mighty foothold to the devil."[143]

This foothold compromises our system when we maintain anger without dealing with it on daily basis. The body systems were not designed to live under the pressure which prevents us from receiving or giving love in our lives.

Determining which area of the body cancer begins to manifest in will tell us what areas of our lives the anger needs to be addressed. For example, if cancer is in the breast, we must examine how past behaviors have prevented us from nurturing the life of God within ourselves and others. This is because nurturing and comforting are what the breasts are for. They also represent the need to take time to nurture the good within ourselves and others as a main part of life. If cancer is in the brain, we must examine how our mind is harboring thoughts of anger, which has prevented us from being loving toward ourselves and others. If cancer is in the colon, we must examine our attachments to false ideas and emotions that we have believed to be true about ourselves or others but are actually false. This is because the job of the colon is to identify and separate the useless error or dross from our system. Instead, the error or dross has become our truth, especially about what we believe about ourselves.

When self-hatred has been infused into our life from guilt, it causes us to believe a lie about our self-worth. This can be instilled from family upbringing, heredity, or a traumatic experience which was never resolved. By subconsciously feeding these thoughts, we cannot but nurture the wounds of things gone wrong because of how we view ourselves. In many cases, it causes us to overwork or help others to the point of neglecting ourselves.

Antidotes for Cancer

Difficulty accessing our feelings because of repression or rejection can cause us to live in an emotionally overwhelmed state for years. Unless the feelings of inner rage are addressed and brought to light, the inability to cope can impair the immune system. Each of us must find our own voice to address these unresolved emotions. Knowing God within ourselves and talking with Him can bring an illuminating light that provides an inner comfort. He can help us discern erroneous ideas that we may have about ourselves. We can seek help from others. Sometimes, conveying how we really feel can shed light to help us identify these damaging thoughts so that we can resolve them. Knowing the truth behind it all can stabilize our mind and body and give us a sense of self-worth, which will restore healing love back into our life.

Addressing our grudges is one way to free ourselves. *The Word of the Lord and the Spirit of the Lord* asks, "What do grudges and hatreds and revenges do? They imprison us. We are being tormented because we hate ourselves. I want you to learn to love yourself. Not the evil self in you but the God in you. So many of us are unaware how much help we need, and we refuse the help God chooses to give us. It is human nature to like people who like you. It is human nature to hate people who hate you. It is divine love from God to love people who hate you and to love people who love you."[144]

When we hate one another, we really hate the part of ourselves that they remind us of. Come up with ways to set these animosities aside and take action to counteract these hatreds. We learn to love God and ourselves by making allowances for another's faults, as they do for our own.

The Skin and the Spiritual Correspondence

The skin is a protective covering or forcefield for the body, which purges us from toxins. It corresponds to the forcefield of energy around our body.

The skin is uniquely defined with some interesting traits in *The Human Body Book*: "The skin is one of the largest organs in the body.... A patch of skin about the size of a fingernail contains 5 million microscopic cells of at least a dozen kinds, 100 sweat glands and their pores, 1000 touch centers, 100–plus hairs with their sebaceous glands up to 3 1/3 ft. (1m) of tiny blood vessels, and about 1 2/3 ft. (0.5 m) of nerve fibers."[145] This shows us how strong the shield of protection is that encases our body and our spirit body. The condition of our skin reveals what is going on inside the thoughts and the emotions of our spirit. How we are really feeling internally will manifest in conditions of our skin.

Spiritual Causes of Skin Cancer

Skin cancer corresponds to vanity, pride, and a superficial lifestyle. Pride loves to gain attention for its own glory and uses appearance, achievement, and self-righteousness to flaunt its self-worth. This false self-image decides its own standards of right and wrong. It lacks sincerity in its pursuit to gain favor and admiration. We say one thing but do another, and our love remains only skin deep.

> "LORD, make me to know mine end,
> and the measure of my days, what it is:
> that I may know how frail I am.
> Behold, thou hast made my days as an handbreadth;
> and mine age is as nothing before thee:
> verily every man at his best state
> is altogether vanity. Selah.
> Surely every man walketh in a vain shew …
> When thou with rebukes
> dost correct man for iniquity,
> thou makest his beauty
> to consume away like a moth:
> surely every man is vanity. Selah."[146]

Antidotes for Skin Cancer

Being real and true to ourselves is more important than gaining admiration. We can accomplish the greatest good by being true to God first and putting ourselves last.

Do good without letting anyone know.

> "Favor is deceitful, and beauty is vain: but a woman that feareth the LORD, she shall be praised."[147]

> "Let us not be desirous of vain glory, provoking one another, envying one another."[148]

When we realize how self-motivated we can become, look for opportunities to be useful without entertaining the ego. When our minds are not glued to selfish motivations, we become freer, more thoughtful, and have greater use for God and others.

Spiritual Causes and Antidotes for Skin Irritations

Results of animosity can create skin conditions such as acne, rashes, eczema, and shingles. When our actions are rash and filled with irritation, the stress begins to manifest through the skin. It becomes irritated so that we can see on the outside what our thoughts and emotions are producing on the inside.

When we see skin irritations, we need to address our reactions to situations that have been angering us. By making a habit of quieting ourselves and taking a step back, we are in a much better state to think clearly under duress. What better way to handle stressful situations that are overwhelming? If we take a deep breath to compose ourselves, we can resist the urge to act on the impulse. We can also roleplay in our mind to see ourselves clearly remaining in control in that situation without letting it affect us. By reinforcing good behaviors internally, we construct a blueprint for our subconscious mind to follow. Maintaining this control elevates our minds to remain at peace without being ruffled by the irritations that surround us daily.

> "Great peace have they which love thy law:
> and nothing shall offend them."[149]

External Skin Irritations: Lice

Lice are parasitic insects that live off human blood by biting the skin. The skin may become sore or infected from scratching. Head lice hatch oval-shaped eggs that attach to the hairs.

Lice can be removed quite easily with a fine-toothed comb and a mild vinegar solution. Bed linens and pillows can be thrown in the dryer for twenty minutes to kill them. Cleanliness, avoiding sharing combs, frequent bathing, and changes of clothing will prevent us from getting them.

Spiritual Correspondences of Lice

Lice correspond to the uncleanliness that is produced when we dishonor God and the truth in our thoughts and actions. Lice usually lodge in the hair, which represents God's honor and glory. Therefore, to have lice is a manifestation of disrespectful thoughts toward God and those in authority, and toward what we know is true and good.

Antidotes for Lice

We free ourselves spiritually by removing habitual thoughts that are dishonoring to God and others. Observe thought patterns and actions that foster these qualities and cast them out. We become spiritually clean by looking for ways to honor God, by doing what is right, and by respecting those in authority.

External Skin Irritations: Ticks

Ticks are another parasite that lives off human blood. Ticks have knife-like tongues that burrow themselves into the outer layer of the skin. A tick needs to be removed completely, the area washed with soap and water, and an antiseptic applied to prevent infection.

Spiritual Causes for Ticks

Ticks live off the blood of others and correspond to habitual biting thoughts and attitudes that we harbor. They penetrate our forcefield and burrow in and hide themselves. These represent hidden motives and intentions that cause us to attach ourselves to others for wrong reasons.

Antidotes for Ticks

Do we have ulterior reasons for our relationships with others? If so, we need to do something to change that. Be aware of using people to further personal agendas or for appearance sake. Look for ways to be true to yourself and honest in your relationships with others.

If we are fueling thoughts of angry remembrances or back-stabbing those we talk about, stop the flow. Refuse to verbalize accusations about others. Pray and extend love toward them, no matter what they have done. (For antidotes for verbal accusations, see chapter 5.)

If there is a problem with recurring tick bites, we may be missing the message. It will keep recurring, like in the movie *Groundhog Day*, until we get the message and change our attitude. When a situation irritates us, God is honoring us because He sees that we are ready to deal with it. He will never give us more than we can handle. That is our moment of opportunity. When we change our attitude toward it, our circumstances will change.

Thou Shalt Not Commit Adultery
Reproductive Organs
Faithfulness

The Seventh Commandment
Figure 10

Chapter 9

The Seventh Commandment

"Thou shalt not commit adultery."
Exodus 20:14; Deuteronomy 5:18

It was not good that Adam should be alone, so God anesthetized him, removed his rib, and made from within him a suitable helper. When he awoke, he acknowledged Eve as part of himself: "This is now bone of my bones, and flesh of my flesh: she shall be called Woman, because she was taken out of Man."[150] Adam was now complete.

Man and woman were created as a part of each other, to live and work together as a team. They were to be co-creators with God and were given dominion over planet earth. The Lord considered them to be one person. We see this idea in Genesis 2, where it says, "They shall be one flesh.... Male and female created he them; and blessed them, and called their name Adam, in the day when they were created."[151] Adam in God's mind had a male side and a female side. He brought this female side out of him so that he could see himself. He could then learn to live in harmony with God and his spirit.

Married Couples in Heaven

Being of "one flesh" comes from a heavenly idea, as we see in *Conjugial Love:* "No married partners can be received into heaven and remain there but such as are inwardly united, or as can be united, as into one; for there two married partners are not called two but one angel."[152]

There is twice as much power between two married people unified with God and each other than there is if they were alone. Jesus said, "If two of you shall agree on earth as touching any thing that they shall ask, it shall be done for them of my Father which is in heaven. For where two or three are gathered together in my name, there am I in the midst of them."[153] God's reality is made known when two minds and hearts are in agreement, and He empowers them both to a greater degree. When married couples are of one mind, they can do the greatest good.

In the book *Conjugial Love*, Emanuel Swedenborg conveys that those in heaven cannot live in the same home unless their loves are similar. "For in the spiritual world, there are not spaces but appearances of space, and these are according to the states of their life, and states of life are according to the states of love. For this reason no one there can dwell in any but his own house, which is provided and assigned to him according to the quality of his love. If he abides elsewhere he labors in the breast and breathing … If they are external inclinations and not at the same time internal, the very house or very place separates, rejects, and expels them. This is the reason why, for those who after preparation are introduced into heaven, a marriage is provided with a consort whose soul so inclines to union with that of the other that they do not desire to be two lives but one. And it is for this reason that after separation a suitable wife is given to the man, and a suitable husband to the woman in like manner."[154] Being of like mind is what draws together those having similar loves in heaven.

Jesus confirmed that once two people are conjoined by God because of their similar loves, they should not be separated by anyone. He said in Matthew, "For this cause shall a man leave father and mother, and shall cleave to his wife: and they twain shall be one flesh? Wherefore they are no more twain, but one flesh. What therefore God hath joined together, let not man put asunder."[155] The word "cleave" in the Hebrew means to follow close or hard after. In order for the man to develop a unified bond with God and his Spirit, he has to be close to his wife. This unity was important enough for God to tell the man to leave his family so that both could learn together how to love each other without additional influences from the family. This kind of love requires a bond of faithfulness and unselfishness.

Faithfulness

The quality that this commandment emphasizes is faithfulness. Because marriage is a covenant of love between a man and a woman, remaining faithful develops the nature of God within each of them. This is accomplished by discipline and remaining loyal and true in thought and deed.

Unselfishness

Unselfishness is the thread of heavenly life that binds married people together. When we are unselfish, we think of the needs of the one we love before ourselves. What they may need may be very different from what we think they need. When we find out what pleases them, we adjust our lives to meet those needs. When each is looking out for the welfare of the other, the needs of both are accommodated. In so doing, a trust is established. This allows the love between them to grow.

In *The Word of the Lord and the Spirit of the Lord,* we are given some advice about unselfishness, which is helpful for a good marriage relationship: "The reason two people can fall in love with each other is because they can see eye to eye. What does it mean to see eye to eye? We both have different eyes, everything, color, construction, the whole works. Attitude, attitude and unselfishness. One must always want to help the other, always. When you detect there's a form of selfishness, you work on it.... Whenever your mother, your wife and your sweetheart asks you for help, notice if you help with having yourself first or you have them first. Most people in a partnership always brush their teeth first. They hardly ever put the toothpaste on their loved one's toothbrush first. They don't help other people first. Do you notice how many times a day you selfishly do something putting yourself first, not the one you love?... Notice also how much of your conduct with your partner is selfish. Whose door to a car do you open first? ... Do you know what this generation lost? Courtesy, etiquette, genuine softness."[156]

Take a moment to evaluate your unselfishness level and look for areas in your life where you can be more thoughtful and sensitive. When you give of yourself in simple ways, you endear yourself to the people who love you.

A good relationship is built on mutual trust. Trust is earned by behavior that is exhibited on a regular basis. Has your behavior earned your wife or husband's trust? Ask them. The answer might be surprising and insightful.

Energy Flow between Married Couples

Energy flow between married couples is very important for health. Continuous conflicts that are not resolved are very oppressive to live with and can break down the defenses of the immune system. Problems can become insurmountable, and illness can set in. Because of this, it is important to set aside regular times to address difficulties when both are in a receptive state and willing to listen to each other. Both need time to honestly express their feelings of what they like and do not like, so they can work together to resolve their differences and accommodate each other's needs. The sooner these needs are expressed and worked on, the better the marriage is long-term. One may need ample space from the other to properly grow in God, strengthening their individual love, connection, and use for Him.

The Effects of Discord: Hindrances to Your Prayers

The scriptures reveal that prayers are hindered because of unresolved conflicts with a spouse. These conflicts result in neglect for the needs of each other. 1 Peter says, "Likewise, ye husbands, dwell with them according to knowledge, giving honour unto the wife, as unto the weaker vessel, and as being heirs together of the grace of life; that your prayers be not hindered."[157] This scripture refers to a tendency in men to be neglectful to their wives: neglect in communication, thoughtful care, and support. These are vital for a unified flow of trust between husband and wife.

The Living Bible puts it this way: "You husbands must be careful of your wives, being thoughtful of their needs and honoring them as the weaker sex. Remember that you and your wife are partners in receiving God's blessings, and if you don't treat her as you should, your prayers will not get ready answers."[158] Think of it: Our own behavior could be preventing our prayers from being answered.

Because of the interchange of energy between a husband and wife, either of them may take on problems or illnesses stemming from the other. God allows this to help us see the things we do not see. Corresponding our spouse's illnesses helps us find a spiritual antidote to deal with the spiritual cause within ourselves. If both help each other to get the message of the illness, there is twice as much power available to combat it.

Reproductive Organs

The seventh commandment governs the reproductive organs because these are the organs we use to either keep or break this commandment. Because this commandment deals with sexual sin in thought and deed, all disharmonies and diseases related to the reproductive organs are affected. If we are not faithful to God's principles in matters of love, we cannot expect to receive the health benefits.

Infertility, miscarriages, fetal deformities, prostate and ovarian disorders, and venereal diseases all reflect blockages of the love of God, which prevents healing from reaching our spirit and body. We may have problems in these areas because of guilt from an abusive relationship or from harboring resentments because we were refused love in life. God's love never stops, but the thoughts and feelings we hold onto can impede His love from reaching us. Once we set our heart to understand the spiritual causes of our illness, we can get to the root of the problem. This way, we can address our emotions and feelings in order to restore the love of God in our lives.

Spiritual Adultery

Jesus identified the spiritual cause of adultery when He said in Matthew, "Ye have heard that it was said by them of old time, Thou shalt not commit adultery: But I say unto you, That whosoever looketh on a woman to lust after her hath committed adultery with her already in his heart."[159] Jesus conveyed that the desire in the heart with intent is tantamount to the act of adultery. Thought and action are not separate. In the spirit world, when we leave our bodies, our thoughts will lead us into instantaneous actions which will either bless or punish us. Jesus wanted us to capture these thoughts (spirits) now while we are in the body so that we could change our tendencies now. That way, they will become minimized and not be a part of our life after death. Jesus's commandment helps us become aware of them, giving us the power to nip them in the bud and cast them from us. Infidelity in mind leads to infidelity in marriage, and Jesus wanted this stopped at its source.

Lust is only concerned about its own gratification. It wants for itself what belongs to another and is really not concerned about the effects on another's life. It can lead to abortion and the creation of single-parent homes. The breaking of marriage vows for sensual pleasure slays even the strongest of men. Honorable men and women who love God will do well to keep their spirit in check, confronting advances and avoiding people whose mind-set condones sleeping around.

Infertility and an Adulterous King

The story in Genesis 20 of Abraham and Sarah conveys the resulting effects on the body when desiring another man's wife. Abimelech, the king of Gerar, wanted Sarah sexually after Abraham told him that she was his sister. This was a half-truth, as Sarah was Abraham's half-sister. The truth that she was Abraham's wife was revealed to Abimelech in a dream; God told him, "Behold, thou art but a dead man, for the woman which thou hast taken; for she is a man's wife."[160] Abimelech spoke to God regarding his innocence: "And God said unto him in a dream, Yea, I know that thou didst this in the integrity of thy heart; for I also withheld thee from sinning against me: therefore suffered I thee not to touch her. Now therefore restore the man his wife; for he is a prophet, and he shall pray for thee, and thou shalt live: and if thou restore her not, know thou that thou shalt surely die, thou, and all that are thine."[161] Abimelech listened to God and returned Sarah back to her husband, as it continues, "So Abraham prayed unto God: and God healed Abimelech, and his wife, and his maidservants; and they bare children. For the LORD had fast closed up all the wombs of the house of Abimelech, because of Sarah Abraham's wife."[162]

The lesson here is twofold. One, God protected both Abraham and Sarah as they sought together by faith to implement His will. Sarah was protected because she was faithful and willing to submit to her husband. Two, the Lord closed up all the wombs in Abimelech's house as a result of his adulterous desire for Sarah. Keep in mind, the king did not actually commit adultery, but the intent to do it created the same consequential effects of infertility as the act itself.

As we see regarding Sarah, God protected her because she was righteous. According to *The Holy Spirit Teachings of God's Original Intention,* "God will always protect a virtuous woman and a righteous woman. If you women want to be protected in your femininity and never be attacked cruelly by any man, remain virtuous. Always remain upright in the marriage duties and in the marriage act. That will always keep you protected by God, if He sees that your attitude in that is always righteous and upright, in every way."[163]

Hannah's Infertility

Hannah's faithfulness and love for God created good fruit in her life. She was one of two wives of the priest, Elkanah. His other wife bore him two sons and daughters. Hannah was repeatedly mocked by her for being infertile when she went up to the temple. Being a God-fearing woman, Hannah prayed to the Lord to have a child. She made a promise that if God answered her prayer, she would give that child to the Lord and consecrate him as a Nazarite for His service. It was an unselfish request that God honored to meet His need in the lives of His people.

Her faithfulness to God created an answer to her prayer. She had a son and named him Samuel and went on to have seven more children. Samuel's name meant "Heard by God." Not only did God hear her prayer, but her son was born with a wonderful gift to hear the voice of God and know the details of future events. Being in love with God who lives within us can produce wonderful gifts in children when they are conceived. These children go on to make God's reality known to others through their unique personalities.

Infertility

Infertility prevents pregnancy from occurring normally. There can be physical problems with the reproductive organs or the fertilization process. There are times when God allows certain blockages to occur for a higher good that we cannot at present understand. Without our knowing, it may not be God's will to have children at a certain time or with a certain person. It is a very personal journey that each of us has to come to terms with. In Sarah's case, she had to wait long after her ability to bear children to have Isaac, while her natural mind grappled with other ways to accomplish this.

Spiritual Causes of Hereditary Infertility

If you were born with a hereditary problem that is preventing pregnancy, the spiritual cause stems from the behaviors of those in your lineage in the areas of love and relationships. Identifying these behaviors in your life and counteracting them will begin to minimize their effects on you. Doing so will assist the mind and body to overcome them in your life. By maintaining the attitude that all things work together for good, you can live a more balanced life, trusting that God is in control of the situation. The results we can only leave in God's hands.

Children after Death

In reality, a young child who dies is never really lost, for we have a loving Father who oversees their care after death. According to *Heaven and Hell,* translated by George Dole, we learn that "as soon as children are reawakened (which happens immediately after their death), they are taken to heaven and given to female angels who have loved children tenderly during their physical lives and had loved God as well … they accept these new ones as their own, and the children love them as their mothers as though this were inborn in them … children are under the direct care of the Lord."[164] It is a comfort to know that these children are very much alive and brought up in His loving care.

Spiritual Causes of Miscarriages and Reproductive Problems

In truth, God does not produce miscarriages or complications in pregnancy. It says in Isaiah, "Shall I bring to the birth, and not cause to bring forth … and shut the womb? saith thy God."[165] God is faithful to us with His promises, but we must remain faithful to Him in our actions to inherit His blessings.

> "As thou knowest not what is the way of the spirit,
> nor how the bones do grow in the womb
> of her that is with child:
> even so thou knowest not
> the works of God who maketh all."[166]

Miscarriages and problems with the reproductive organs occur because habitual wrong choices have been made either by the individual or those in the hereditary line. Unfaithfulness to God's love and truth separates us from Him, causing the Spirit of God to become diminished in these areas. As a result, our life cannot produce adequate fruit. When this is done habitually over a period of time through the same hereditary line, the potency of the DNA and cellular life is actually changed, creating disruptive energy and blockages in the reproductive organs. When thoughts and actions are habitually self-centered, we unknowingly create separations from the love of God. A divided mind that is not faithful to God or one's spouse interrupts the flow of the Spirit of God to the reproductive organs.

Antidotes for Miscarriages and Reproductive Problems

Our job is to reverse this hereditary, downhill spiral by living lives in obedience to the Spirit of truth.

> "Delight thyself also in the LORD;
> and he shall give thee the desires of thine heart.
> Commit thy way unto the LORD;
> trust also in him;
> and he shall bring it to pass."[167]

God will bless a heart that is single-minded and faithful to what is good and true in His sight. The blessings of a fruitful life will follow and accompany the delivery as well.

> "She shall be saved in childbearing, if they
> continue in faith and charity
> and holiness with sobriety."[168]

There is nothing more important to God than the union of a soul with His mind and heart. His love longs for us to see things from the light of heaven so that we can have an attitude change. In this way, we partner with God by allowing Him to reveal to us how to overcome these hereditary deficiencies in our lives. In so doing, we can reap the many blessings He has to give. "Marrying" God means that we want to become one with Him and His truth by living it. There is a feeable emanation from those who do this. God is a faithful friend who sticks closer than a brother. It is His love and truth that is an anchor for our soul through difficult times.

> "The truth changes nobody until they marry it
> and love it and it is their life.
> Then you will have the fruit of the Spirit.
> One of the things of the fruit of the Spirit is
> you are not afraid,
> you have courage and you have a joy."[169]

Uterine Fibroids

According to *The Human Body Book,* "Non-cancerous tumors that occur within the wall of the uterus are called, fibroids. They can occur singly or in groups and range in size from pea-sized to as large as a grapefruit."[170] When there are obstructions in the uterus, we have to take a look at what the uterus represents so that we can understand the spiritual meaning of fibroids.

Spiritual Correspondence of the Uterus and Uterine Fibroids

The uterus corresponds to the place where the innocent thoughts and feelings of God are developed and nourished. It is a place where love allows another human being to grow. When fibroids obstruct the uterus, it corresponds to restricted emotions and thoughts toward the love of God, especially in the area of love and relationships. Fibroids reveal a habitual pattern of denying innocent feelings and thoughts of love because of prideful resentments. Pride and resentment are something we choose. They become a part of our spirit because we let them in. They are not a part of our true, God-given self. According to *You Can Heal Your Life*, fibroid tumors and cysts are caused by "nursing a hurt from a partner" or "rejecting femininity."[171]

Antidotes for Uterine Fibroids

We have to look at areas where we have rejected the love of God in our relationships and restore it by loving ourselves (and others) despite our circumstances. This means addressing grudges and hurts from our past that have robbed us of our self-worth. We do this by being honest about what we really feel in our relationships with others. Once we pinpoint the resentments that have held us back from being true to God within ourselves and others, we can begin making steps to separate from these negative feelings by replacing them with loving actions through principle and prayer.

When we feel the reactions of pride separating us from the love of God, we need to identify it and disengage ourselves from it. Purposefully direct loving actions with calmness toward the person who is irritating or hurting you. In order to override negative reactions, we need to principle ourselves, despite how we feel. We can calmly disengage our tension by breathing in and not giving in to our feelings. Take a step back, respond with self-control, and be willing to listen as well as respond. This will not only diffuse our reactions but temper the reactions of those we are speaking to. People tend to react to the same emotional reactions that we put out. Communication is a big key toward freeing blocked-up energies in married life.

Venereal Diseases

Venereal diseases are infections passed from person to person, usually through promiscuous sexual activity. Gonorrhea can spread to other parts of the body and cause infertility. Syphilis, if left untreated, can lead to mental illness, nervous system disorders, and even death. These diseases are generally the result of lustful or adulterous lifestyles and sleeping around.

Spiritual Causes of Venereal Diseases

Generally speaking, venereal diseases reflect unfaithfulness to God and adulterating what is true in matters of love and relationships. When we adulterate something, we put no difference between what is good and what is evil. We call good evil and evil good. This confusion occurs because of unregulated, excessive emotions that have no desire to know or apply the truth.

Antidotes for Venereal Diseases

"This I say then, Walk in the Spirit, and ye shall not fulfill the lust of the flesh. For the flesh lusteth against the Spirit, and the Spirit against the flesh: and these are contrary the one to the other: so that ye cannot do the things that ye would.... Now the works of the flesh are manifest, which are these; Adultery, fornication, uncleanness, lasciviousness ... I have also told you in time past, that they which do such things shall not inherit the kingdom of God.... And they that are Christ's have crucified the flesh with the affections and lusts."[172]

"For this is the will of God, even your sanctification, that ye should abstain from fornication."[173]

"For he that soweth to his flesh shall of the flesh reap corruption; but he that soweth to the Spirit shall of the Spirit reap life everlasting."[174]

"Only acknowledge thine iniquity, that thou hast transgressed against the LORD thy God, and hast scattered thy ways to the strangers under every green tree, and ye have not obeyed my voice, saith the LORD. Turn, O backsliding children, saith the LORD; for I am married unto you.... And I will give you pastors according to mine heart, which shall feed you with knowledge and understanding."[175]

"Flee also youthful lusts: but follow righteousness, faith, charity, peace, with them that call on the Lord out of a pure heart."[176]

Hang out with those who have a love for God, goodness, and truth. Do not go along with what everyone else is calling good. This will keep you spiritual and healthy.

"Lust not after her beauty in thine heart; neither let her take thee with her eyelids. For by means of a whorish woman a man is brought to a piece of bread: and the adulteress will hunt for the precious life. Can a man take fire in his bosom, and his clothes not be burned? Can one go upon hot coals, and his feet not be burned? So he that goeth in to his neighbour's wife; whosoever toucheth her shall not be innocent."[177]

Keep your distance from women whose only motive is to use you for sex. Selling yourself out for a moment's pleasure has internal consequences and steals your God-given life.

"That is why I say to run from sex sin. No other sin affects the body as this one does. When you sin this sin it is against your own body. Haven't you yet learned that your body is the home of the Holy Spirit God gave you, and that he lives within you? Your own body does not belong to you. For God has bought you with a great price. So use every part of your body to give glory back to God, because he owns it." [178]

Thou Shalt Not Steal
Eyes, Hands, and Feet
Generous and Good

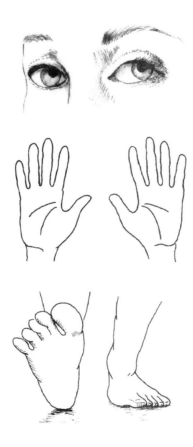

The Eighth Commandment
Figure 11

Chapter 10

The Eighth Commandment

"Thou shalt not steal."
Exodus 20:15; Deuteronomy 5:19

When we steal from another, the life of God is robbed from us, producing a lack of abundance and health in our own life. In reality, we are stealing from God, who is the giver of all things. As a result, we set in motion a reaping that causes others to steal our goods as well. Taking something that does not belong to us reveals a discontentment in life and a selfish disregard for the possessions of another. Today, stealing and pilfering the goods of others is often done brazenly, without conscience, in broad daylight.

All our works are recorded in the annals of life. Whatever thefts we have committed will be revealed after death. The scriptures teach that a thief cannot enter heaven. This is because selfishness has become our life and is contrary to the life lived in heaven. God looks at the motive of the heart when a deed is done and always takes that into consideration. In the book *Heaven and Hell,* translated by George Dole, it speaks of stealing after death: "There were people who had deceived others with malicious skill and had stolen from them. Their deceptions and thefts were also recounted one after the other, many of them known to practically no one in the world other than themselves. They even admitted them because they were made plain as day, along with every thought, intention, pleasure, and fear that mingled in their minds at the time…. In a word, all their evils, crimes, thefts, wiles, and deceptions are made clear to every evil spirit. They are drawn from their own memories and exposed. There is no room for denial because all the circumstances are presented together."[179]

Acts of stealing that are not rectified in this life follow us after death, for the spirit of stealing dwells within our spirit body. Because we did not resist the inclination to steal or repay items stolen in life, this spirit remains within and brings us after death into the selfish hell that it created. This is because it became a part of our nature through our freewill choice. The habitual decisions that we make now are woven into the fiber of our being and stay within us unless we get them out now.

The act of stealing, whether done in thought or deed, affects the health of our hands, feet, and eyes, for these are the parts that we use to keep or break this commandment. The eyes see the things that we want to steal. The hands take them, and the feet walk away with them. When we steal, we diminish the energy fields to these areas of the body. Diseases, accidents, and problems with these parts should alert us to the corresponding cause of stealing, whether done naturally or spiritually. These problems occur not because God wills it, but because we are reaping for our own choices or the actions of those in our hereditary line.

Stealing the Enemies' Goods

The story in Joshua 7 conveys how God's protection and power are removed when items are stolen. Achan was a man who during an Israeli battle stole the goods of the enemy that he was fighting. He hid them in the ground under his tent. These goods consisted of gold, silver, and a Babylonian garment. This act caused Israel to be defeated by their enemy at Ai. The LORD informed Joshua that the theft had taken place and was the reason why the battle had been lost. He told Joshua that unless he searched out and destroyed the culprit, His presence ensuring future victories would be removed.

> "Therefore the children of Israel could not stand
> before their enemies ... because they were accursed:
> neither will I be with you any more,
> except ye destroy the accursed thing
> from among you."[180]

The lesson here is that stealing removed God's blessing and protection from the Israeli army. Until the theft was rectified, God's power would not accompany them to win future battles. So, too, when we have stolen goods in our possession, we prevent God's power from assisting us fully in life.

One way we can restore this power back into our lives is to search out and remove stolen items in our possession and return them to their rightful owners. If they are no longer in our possession, we should contact the owner and offer monetary value for it. If it is impossible to compensate the owner, give the comparable amount to someone in need.

God is a God of the little things, whether it is a quarter, a dime, or a hair tie. These are all possessions that are a part of someone's life. They are significant in the eyes of God. Simple items in our possession have auras from the owners within and around them. This is why Paul's handkerchiefs could heal, for his life of living the truth was in them (Acts 19:12). Every jot and tittle in the Word of God has meaning and value (Matthew 5:18); so does the smallest application of it in our life.

"For who hath despised the day of small things?"[181]

As a teenager, I stole items from different stores. I learned this truth and made rectification for them; I wrote letters to the stores' owners, explaining my previous thefts, and offered the full cost of the items with any additional expenses that had incurred over time. In all cases, they forgave the debt and were glad to get such a letter. This helped clear my slate with God and allowed God's power to enter my life in a new way.

When we make rectification, the energies to the hands, feet, and eyes are restored. The way we are free from the spirit of stealing is through a spirit of giving. Giving unselfishly has its own reward internally.

Types of Natural Stealing

Below are some different examples of stealing. See if you have done any of these in your life. If so, come up with a personal plan of how you can repay:

- overcharging on labor in business
- exacting improper interest on loaned money
- evading taxes
- neglecting to repay debts
- falsifying business accounts
- neglecting to tithe
- plagiarizing
- borrowing items without returning them
- damaging borrowed items without offering to replace them
- mooching off of friends for favors in the name of brotherly kindness
- sneaking into movie theaters, amusement parks, and so on without paying
- underpaying employees
- stealing time from people by being lazy, negligent, or late
- leaving the job early when being paid for a full day
- making more money than a partner in business who is doing more work than you
- stealing identities
- kidnapping
- bribing or accepting bribes
- embezzling
- establishing false charities

Spiritual Stealing: Distorting Good and Truth for Selfish Motives

Jesus said, "He that entereth not by the door into the sheepfold, but climbeth up some other way, the same is a thief and a robber.… All that ever came before me are thieves and robbers.… The thief cometh not, but for to steal, and to kill, and to destroy: I am come that they might have life, and that they might have it more abundantly."[182] Jesus is clarifying here that thieves can rob the truth, which prevents it from being implemented. This is because of a lack of genuine desire to hear the truth or a belief in teachings that are not scripturally founded. In either case, the truth is stolen, by being distorted and used for selfish motives. It then becomes a counterfeit, pawned off as the original to deceive the listeners.

The scriptures warn us to turn away from those who appear to have truth but have no power. This is so because they are not living the truth of their message.

> "For men shall be lovers of their own selves ...
> having a form of godliness, but denying the
> power thereof: from such turn away."[183]

God's power will always accompany real truth that is being practiced in life by a teacher. The power Jesus gave was for the purpose of overcoming human nature by keeping the commandments that He taught. In this way, we could subdue the negativity of our nature and conquer the resulting effects of sickness and disease.

Spiritual Stealing: Self-Recognition

Wanting recognition and not giving credit to God for good works that are done through us are forms of spiritual stealing. Every gift that we have been given comes from God, and we should honor Him for it. In *The Word of the Lord and the Spirit of the Lord*, we see a new perspective on self-recognition: "Because you take credit for the goodness that is done in and through you, you are a plagiarist, you are a robber, you steal.... That is why it is hard to find a real Christian because every person wants recognition and nobody in heaven has recognition, only God.... When you want an identity, you open hell and it comes in and heaven is closed. Nobody in heaven has an identity, only God. Only God is good.... The reason why many of you are blocked in your income and in the payment of your bills is because you have the spirit of stealing in you and God wants to free you."[184] Using our energy to maintain an image of ourselves is one way to lose power in our lives naturally, spiritually, and financially. When motives are not right with God, it will always produce a lack of abundance.

In contrast, heaven can be opened when we refuse credit for the good that we do, realizing that we are just servants of God's goodness. We can do this by doing things humbly, for the love of being useful, without show or desiring accolades. When we honor God this way, we free ourselves from the spirit of stealing. This restores the flow of power to our eyes, hands, and feet. Letting go of self-recognition is how to have the greatest power flow in the human body.

In *Heaven and Hell*, translated by George Dole, we gain an enlightening perspective on how a life of self-recognition affects people after death: "Spirits who during their earthly lives had convinced themselves that they were the sources of the good they did and the truth they believed, or who had claimed these virtues as their own, are not accepted into heaven. This is the belief of all those who place merit in good deeds and claim to be righteous. Angels avoid them. They regard them as stupid and as thieves–stupid because they are constantly looking at themselves and not at the Divine, and thieves because they take from the Lord what is actually his. They stand in opposition to heaven's belief that the Lord's divine nature in angels is what makes heaven."[185]

In the following pages, we will address the spiritual correspondences of the hands, eyes, and feet, as well as the antidotes for problems that affect them.

Spiritual Correspondences of the Hands and Arms

The aura of both of our hands contains a record of all our works. These works are imprinted on our hands. Because the hands are what we work with, how we work is reflected in the condition of our hands. They convey what we do and what we hold onto or trust in. The hands can be used to take things that do not belong to us or be used to give unselfishly to others. In *Heaven and Hell*, translated by George Dole, we see how angels access our life's works after death: "When we are being faced with our deeds after death, angels who have been given the task of examining look searchingly into the face and continue their examination through the whole body, beginning with the fingers first of one hand and then of the other and continuing through the whole."[186] The fingers of our spiritual hands convey to them all of the works that we have done in our body.

Another version of *Heaven and Hell* conveys that our arms and hands reflect the power of our works: "Moreover, the power of the whole man passes into the arms, and by means of these the whole body exercises its powers. It is for this reason that in the Word 'arms' and 'hand' signify powers."[187]

The hands also represent our abilities. Our right hand corresponds to abilities that are used for what is good, and our left hand corresponds to abilities that are used for what is true. Determining which hand we have a problem with will help us learn the spiritual cause. If we have a problem with our right hand, it reveals there is a problem with our motives in doing what is good. If we have a problem with our left hand, it reveals that there are false standards that we are holding onto in doing what we think is right.

Below is a list of scriptural antidotes that assist with healing hand problems and injuries:

Antidotes for Hand Problems/Injuries

"Honour the LORD with thy substance, and with the firstfruits of all thine increase: so shall thy barns be filled with plenty, and thy presses shall burst out with new wine."[188]

"Don't withhold repayment of your debts. Don't say 'some other time,' if you can pay now."[189]

"The lazy man longs for many things but his hands refuse to work. He is greedy to get, while the godly love to give!"[190]

"If your hand does wrong, cut it off. Better live forever with one hand than be thrown into the unquenchable fires of hell with two!"[191]

It is better to identify the motivating spirit that is causing you to steal and get rid of it than to have that spirit remain within you and bring you into its hell after death. Cut it off by casting it out and restoring what you have taken. By freeing yourself this way, heaven and its healing energy will have access to you.

"Let him that stole steal no more: but rather let him labour, working with his hands the thing which is good, that he may have to give to him that needeth."[192]

Do not charge interest to a friend who wants to borrow money from you.

"If someone demands your coat, give him your shirt besides. Give what you have to anyone who asks you for it; and when things are taken away from you, don't worry about getting them back. Treat others as you want them to treat you. Do you think you deserve credit for merely loving those who love you? Even the godless do that! And if you do good only to those who do you good—is that so wonderful?"[193]

"And that ye study to be quiet, and to do your own business, and to work with your own hands, as we commanded you; that ye may walk honestly toward them that are without, and that ye may have lack of nothing."[194]

"This should be your ambition: to live a quiet life, minding your own business and doing your own work.... As a result, people who are not Christians will trust and respect you, and you will not need to depend on others for enough money to pay your bills."[195]

"Will a man rob God? Yet ye have robbed me. But ye say, Wherein have we robbed thee? In tithes and offerings.... Bring ye all the tithes into the storehouse, that there may be meat in mine house, and prove me now herewith, saith the LORD of hosts, if I will not open you the windows of heaven, and pour you out a blessing, that there shall not be room enough to receive it."[196]

The Eyes

According to *The Human Body Book,* "Eyesight provides the brain with more input than all other senses combined. Each optic nerve contains one million nerve fibers, and it is estimated that more than half of the information in the conscious mind enters through the eyes."[197] When light comes into the eye from the cornea, the image that we see is upside down when it reaches the retina at the back of the eye. In the retina are millions of rods and cones. These send electrical impulses of the image to the optic nerves of each eye, which then go to the brain, where the images are turned right side up.

Spiritual Correspondence of the Eyes

The eyes correspond to our understanding and our perception. Because eyesight provides more information to our brain than all the other senses, we can see how important our perception is for the health of the body. How we perceive something has a great influence on the effectiveness of the energy flow to the eyes. If we see things with a good and right attitude, energies flow freely to the eyes. If we perceive something good from God's perspective as something bad, it causes the energies to the eyes to become depleted, creating energy blockages to the spiritual eyes that materialize in eye problems. Perceiving incorrectly creates an anxiety that mischannels energy to the eye. This anxiety can cause eye pressures to rise. When these conditions are prolonged, it can damage the optic nerve and eventually damage our vision. Everything stems from how we perceive something. Eye problems in general correspond to a false perception of what is good and true.

According to *Physiological Correspondences,* "the left eye corresponds to the understanding of what is true, and the right eye to the understanding of what is good."[198] If we have problems with our right eye, we have a wrong understanding of what is good. If we have problems with our left eye, we have a wrong understanding of what is true. We are using false standards and emotions in how we perceive.

When we have an erroneous view of a thing instead of God's perspective, it darkens our spiritual understanding and prevents healing to our eyes. When our own desires become our standard instead of the truth, we confuse evil with good and good with evil without realizing it. Before eye problems materialize, these problems begin in the realm of spirit, where our thoughts are conjoined with a desire that we believe to be good. We act upon it, and it becomes our truth. Because it may not be the actual truth, a veil will remain upon the heart and mind's eye. This veil prevents us from identifying the error we believe in and hinders the healing process. This in time will manifest in the corresponding eye problems to show us that our spiritual perception is being blocked and dimmed.

> "By ... seeing ye shall see, and shall not perceive:
> for this people's heart is waxed gross,
> and their ears are dull of hearing,
> and their eyes they have closed;
> lest at any time they should see with their eyes,
> and hear with their ears,
> and should understand with their heart,
> and should be converted,
> and I should heal them."[199]

Truth will either unveil us or blind us, depending upon our attitude. It is our choice to either remain in error or to see clearly. Jesus clarified His mission regarding our perception when He said, "For judgment I am come into this world, that they which see not might see; and that they which see might be made blind. And some of the Pharisees which were with him heard these words and said unto him, 'Are we blind also?' Jesus said unto them, If ye were blind, ye should have no sin: but now ye say, We see; therefore your sin remaineth."[200]

When we are able to see our blindness, we become unveiled to the error of our thinking, which will frees us. If we cannot see our error, we will insist that we can see correctly. Our own denial will prevent our healing. We see clearly by getting God's mind from the source of light that comes from the Word of God.

> "The entrance of thy words giveth light;
> it giveth understanding unto the simple."[201]

Truth enlightens our mind and gives us a higher understanding with a clarity that we would not receive on our own. As a result, veils are removed from our spiritual eyes, and we understand things from a higher elevation and perspective. Truth from scripture quickens our spirit and strengthens the energy fields to the eyes. This provides us with a new perspective and a renewed hope. Good and truth can enter our hearts, enabling us to value ourselves in a new light.

When we are in the dark about an issue, our joy is lost, and we feel the heaviness that accompanies it. This is the veil that error produces. When our intentions are wrong, our vision and judgment become clouded. We walk in darkness, and answers to life's problems do not come quickly.

Spiritual Causes of Nearsightedness

The spiritual cause for nearsightedness, according to *God Can Heal You,* is "lacking vision [long range]; foresight; worldliness; lust."[202] Nearsightedness causes us to be unable to see far. This condition manifests when we focus only on the present, which can cause us to be overindulgent in the present pleasures of the world, with its appearances and lusts. If we can identify how this perspective is affecting us, we will gain greater insight into how our minds operate.

Antidotes for Nearsightedness

"A wise man is cautious and avoids danger; a fool plunges ahead with great confidence."[203]

Never be so sure of yourself that you throw common sense to the wind.

"A wise man thinks ahead; a fool doesn't, and even brags about it!"[204]

Being rash causes us to do everything last minute, regardless of the effects it has on others. Thinking ahead helps us avoid problems and prevents us from taking advantage of others.

> "O that they were wise, that they understood this, that
> they would consider their latter end!"[205]

The decisions we make now will cause us to either gain or lose opportunities for a heavenly life.

> "He that hasteth to be rich hath an evil eye, and
> considereth not that poverty shall come upon him."[206]

Evaluating our spiritual priorities will lead us in the right direction.

> "A prudent man foresees the difficulties ahead and
> prepares for them; the simpleton goes blindly on and
> suffers the consequences."[207]

Spiritual Causes of Farsightedness

According to *God Can Heal You,* farsightedness corresponds to the "failure to give present truth and present situations proper importance."[208] Farsightedness prevents us from being able to see near and what is of primary spiritual importance. We have problems with applying God's messages to life's situations. This creates a veiled state of mind, affecting our vision. We are putting too much emphasis on future fears, which is preventing us from using present truth that we know with an elevated, spiritual mind. We have become natural minded about planning for the future and miss present opportunities for usefulness.

Antidotes for Farsightedness

> "But if your eye is clouded with evil thoughts and desires,
> you are in deep spiritual darkness. And oh, how deep
> that darkness can be! You cannot serve two masters: God
> and money. For you will hate one and love the other, or
> else the other way around.... So don't worry at all about
> having enough food and clothing.... But your heavenly
> Father already knows perfectly well that you need them,

and he will give them to you if you give him first place in your life and live as he wants you to. So don't be anxious about tomorrow. God will take care of your tomorrow too. Live one day at a time."[209]

"Lay not up for yourselves treasures upon earth, where moth and rust doth corrupt, and where thieves break through and steal: but lay up for yourselves treasures in heaven, where neither moth nor rust doth corrupt, and where thieves do not break through nor steal: for where your treasure is, there will your heart be also."[210]

"The way of a fool is right in his own eyes: but he that hearkeneth unto counsel is wise."[211]

"Be not wise in thine own eyes: fear the LORD, and depart from evil. It shall be health to thy navel, and marrow to thy bones."[212]

Macular Degeneration

The macula portion of the eye over time can degenerate from heredity, aging, or improper diet. The macula is responsible for fine-tune vision. Macular degeneration does not affect peripheral vision or seeing in color.

At the time of this writing, I was diagnosed with the beginning of macular degeneration. My ophthalmologist has told me that having the symptoms does not always mean it gets worse to the point of blindness. It varies by individual. I was told to add dark green and orange vegetables and fruits to my diet to assist with the condition. www.naturaleyecare.com lists some additional nutritional supplements that have been documented to prevent additional eye damage. My mother had this problem, and in her nineties, she was legally blind in both eyes. Even though this is a hereditary problem, I have the choice of not allowing the behavior that causes this condition to rob my vision, as well. The behaviors that accompany this condition are stronger in me, since they come through the hereditary line from birth.

Conditions like this are presented for us to identify and overcome the corresponding behavior. The best we can do is to target them and feed the eye with the right attitude, perception, and nutrition. The rest is in God's hands.

Spiritual Causes and Antidotes for Macular Degeneration

In simple terms, the spiritual cause of macular degeneration is hypocritical judging: blaming others for their faults but not identifying them within ourselves. Human nature is such that it is easier to blame others for their faults than to deal with our own weaknesses.

Seeing ourselves means that we are willing to be honest and be shown that our perspective is wrong. Jesus gave us an applicable remedy about this when He said,

> "And why beholdest thou
> the mote that is in thy brother's eye,
> but considerest not the beam
> that is in thine own eye?
> Or how wilt thou say to thy brother,
> Let me pull out the mote out of thine eye;
> and, behold, a beam is in thine own eye?
> Thou hypocrite,
> first cast out the beam out of thine own eye;
> and then shalt thou see clearly
> to cast the mote out of thy brother's eye."[213]

Looking to blame others or situations outside of ourselves will create a mote or impairment in our eye. Take note that the beam in our eye is larger than the mote that we see in another's eye. When we acknowledge our own faults, blame toward others begins to dissipate. Doing a kindness or praying for them diminishes the mesmerizing effects that their faults have made on us. The secret is not to focus on them.

"Love ... is not irritable or touchy. It does not hold grudges and will hardly even notice when others do it wrong."[214]

Spiritual Correspondences of the Feet

Because our feet move and cause us to take action, it would follow that our feet correspond to our willingness to act on the truth that we know. Our right foot corresponds to the application of goodness in our lives, and our left foot corresponds to our application of truth.

All of the nerves governing the organs in our body are located in our feet. The way we walk, naturally and spiritually, affects the health of all of our organs. When we walk in truth by applying it, we are freed from the negativity of our human nature. A sense of peace fills our spirit because of the goodness it provides. When we walk in error, we lose that peace.

"How beautiful upon the mountains
are the feet of him that bringeth good tidings,
that publisheth peace;
that bringeth good tidings of good,
that publisheth salvation."[215]

Spiritual Causes of Foot Problems

According to *God Can Heal You,* feet problems correspond to "walking according to one's own [false] standards ... unreliableness; causing mischief; intermeddling into the affairs of others."[216] When we walk after our own ways without consulting God, our feet are affected. Swelling feet correspond to walking in pride. If our right foot has a problem, it is a warning that we are not walking right with God. If our left foot has a problem, we have stronger habits of not walking right that have become our standard. God speaks to us through our feet so that we can see when we are out of the way and not following His voice in our daily decisions.

It is God's love that allows problems with our feet for our good. In reality, our own patterns of thinking and walking create foot problems and injuries. God hopes that we can make the application for change so that we can walk in a higher spiritual light. This will allow angelic forces to return to us and protect our feet.

> "For he shall give his angels charge over thee,
> to keep thee in all thy ways.
> They shall bear thee up in their hands,
> lest thou dash thy foot against a stone."[217]

The Story of Balaam in Numbers 22

The story of Balaam gives us an example of how our actions can cause situations to affect our feet. Balaam saddled his donkey and left with the princes of Moab, after being bribed with promotion and wealth to curse Israel. God told him not to go because His people were blessed. He proceeded to go anyway, riding upon his donkey. An angel blocked Balaam's way between two walls but was not seen by him. When the donkey saw the angel, she pushed herself against the wall, crushing Balaam's foot. After going further and being struck by Balaam's staff many times, the Lord opened the donkey's mouth. She reminded him that she had never been unfaithful in getting him where he needed to go. Then the Lord opened Balaam's eyes to see the angel standing in the way with his drawn sword. Balaam bowed his head and fell flat on his face.

The angel said, "Wherefore hast thou smitten thine ass these three times? behold, I went out to withstand thee, because thy way is perverse before me."[218]

Balaam's actions defied listening to what he knew was right and led to circumstances that injured his foot.

When we exert our own will against the will of God, things do not work out, and injuries occur to our feet to show us to ourselves. Balaam had heard what God had told him but would not do it. His refusal to comply with God's inspiration caused his foot to be injured.

> Watch for signs.
> Consult God and change direction
> when your path is being blocked.

When we are delayed in life, we must see it as God's intervention and leading for us that day. We can learn a little more about this in *The Word of the Lord and the Spirit of the Lord*: "Are you killing, grieving, crushing God and His Spirit within you by the places that you go to? ... He's put a power on your body to delay. You want to break through the delay.... God doesn't want you to go to that place. He's delayed you. It looks like it's you, and of course you can't be delayed. So you broke through that block.... Then God lets certain mild accidents happen to you, that will prevent you from getting to that place, and you get frustrated and angry because you've got to go to that place. It never occurs to you, God doesn't want me there. Not today."[219] Understanding detours and blocks as coming from God for our good sets us on a road to greater love and trust in Him and healing for our feet.

Antidotes for Foot Problems

"Behold, I send an Angel before thee, to keep thee in the way, and to bring thee into the place which I have prepared. Beware of him, and obey his voice, provoke him not; for he will not pardon your transgressions: for my name is in him. But if thou shalt indeed obey his voice, and do all that I speak; then I will be an enemy unto thine enemies, and an adversary unto thine adversaries."[220]

"And thine ears shall hear a word behind thee, saying, This is the way, walk ye in it, when ye turn to the right hand, and when ye turn to the left."[221]

"He that trusteth in his own heart is a fool: but whoso walketh wisely, he shall be delivered."[222]

"I have refrained my feet from every evil way, that I might keep thy word. Thy word is a lamp unto my feet, and a light unto my path."[223]

"Keep sound wisdom and discretion: so shall they be life unto thy soul, and grace to thy neck. Then shalt thou walk in thy way safely, and thy foot shall not stumble."[224]

"Withdraw thy foot from thy neighbour's house; lest he be weary of thee, and so hate thee. Confidence in an unfaithful man in time of trouble is like a broken tooth, and a foot out of joint."[225]

"And make straight paths for your feet, lest that which is lame be turned out of the way; but let it rather be healed. Follow peace with all men, and holiness, without which no man shall see the Lord."[226]

"The steps of a good man are ordered by the LORD: and he delighteth in his way. He is ever merciful, and lendeth; and his seed is blessed."[227]

Generosity: An Antidote

Generosity is the quality to develop for healing of the eyes, hands, and feet. Incorporating generosity combats the selfishness of human nature that inspires us to steal another's goods and selfishly hold onto things that we should let go of. When we give unselfishly without thought for ourselves, we become an empty channel for God's abundant life to enter and fill us. This power and life strengthens the natural flow of energy to our eyes, our hands, and our feet. When we give of ourselves (not just our material possessions), we are truly giving.

"He which soweth sparingly
shall reap also sparingly;
and he which soweth bountifully
shall reap also bountifully.
Every man according as he purposeth in his heart,
so let him give;

not grudgingly, or of necessity:
for God loveth a cheerful giver."[228]

The Living Bible says, "Every one must make up his own mind as to how much he should give. Don't force anyone to give more than he really wants to, for cheerful givers are the ones God prizes. God is able to make it up to you by giving you everything you need and more, so that there will not only be enough for your own needs, but plenty left over to give joyfully to others. It is as the scriptures say: 'The godly man gives generously to the poor. His good deeds will be an honor to him forever.' Yes, God will give you much so that you can give away much, and when we take your gifts to those who need them they will break out into thanksgiving and praise to God for your help. So, two good things happen as a result of your gifts: those in need are helped, and they overflow with thanks to God. Those you help will be glad not only because of your generous gifts to themselves and to others, but they will praise God for this proof that your deeds are as good as your doctrine."[229]

I went to California as a teenager and learned a lesson about letting go of possessions. I had purchased some jewelry at a local store, which I put in the pocket of my green windbreaker jacket. I went up to a hillside covered with golden, dry grass and sat there enjoying the immense beauty of the mountainside. I laid down and immersed myself in the moment of an elevated state of beauty and love, which seemed almost timeless. After a while, I realized that the jewelry had fallen out of my pocket and gotten lost in the field somewhere. I became so upset, because it was a souvenir of a place that I really loved. I sat down for a moment as the thoughts swirled in my heart. I wrestled within myself and then made the conscious decision to let go of it. I realized that the peace and love that I had encountered on that hillside were more important to me than what I had purchased. Because I loved those mountains and wanted to maintain the peace, beauty and love of that place within me, I accepted giving up my prized possession. I looked at it as a gift to the hills that I loved.

Unconditional love is about giving up what we love the most. In it holds a gem: a true joy. Life is not about getting. It is about giving and giving generously. What we desire will someday be removed from us and be given to someone else. In giving up what we love now, we find the true essence of our life. In this way, we find out more about who God is within us. There is nothing material that can separate us from that love once we find it.

> "It is possible to give away and become richer!
> It is also possible to hold on too tightly
> and lose everything.
> Yes, the liberal man shall be rich!
> By watering others, he waters himself."[230]

When you are in need, it is time to give something away. The law of supply and demand works that way. If we find ourselves in a place where our natural needs are not being met, we can be sure that some sort of selfishness or stealing (natural or spiritual) is present. For we have this promise from our Creator:

> "Give, and it shall be given unto you;
> good measure, pressed down, and shaken together,
> and running over, shall men give into your bosom.
> For with the same measure that ye mete
> withal it shall be measured to you again....
> Give to every man that asketh of thee;
> and of him that taketh away thy goods
> ask them not again.
> And if ye lend to them of whom ye hope to receive,
> what thank have ye?
> for sinners also lend to sinners,
> to receive as much again.
> But love ye your enemies, and do good, and lend,
> hoping for nothing again;
> and your reward shall be great,
> and ye shall be the children of the Highest:
> for he is kind unto the unthankful
> and to the evil."[231]

Thou Shalt Not
Bear False Witness
Mouth and Ears
Truthfulness

The Ninth Commandment
Figure 12

Chapter 11

The Ninth Commandment

"Thou shalt not bear false witness against thy neighbour."
Exodus 20:16; Deuteronomy 5:20

The scriptures teach that it is impossible for God to lie. By commanding us not to lie, God is inviting us to be like Him. When we live like God, we have greater access to heavenly life within ourselves. We cannot enter into it if we have made a lifestyle of lying to ourselves or others.

Lying to protect ourselves will separate us from God and will set in motion disharmonies that affect our mouth and ears. This is because lying is done with the mouth and is heard by the ears. In order to prevent these disharmonies, we must look within to uncover areas in our life where we are lying and correct it. We begin this important step by being completely honest with ourselves about how we feel. With the ears we need to hear the truth, and with the mouth we need to express it.

When God told Adam not to eat of the tree in the garden, it was for his good and for his protection. He did not need to know the details of why or wonder about it to decide if it would be good or not. The command that God gave him had in it all the goodness and blessings that Adam needed if he obeyed it. This command was given to him before God created Eve. God wanted the simplicity and faith in Adam's mind to keep His word despite any outward advice. Once Eve's faith was diluted by questioning the validity of God's Word, Satan was able to inspire her to disobey and convince Adam as well.

The First Lie

The serpent's denial of the Word of God was the first lie told. He directly lied to Eve, when he contradicted God's words and said, "Ye shall not surely die."[232] God had told Adam that in the day he ate from the tree, he would surely die. This was the beginning of a spiritual death, a separation from God. By using her mind to analyze, Eve overrode the simplicity of the truth and began to discredit it. The blame game started as to who was at fault when God questioned them. God enforced the consequences of disobeying Him, beginning with a curse on the serpent.

According to *The Holy Spirit Teachings of God's Original Intention*, "The devil only plays on thoughts that question God's Word, that challenge God's Word. Once you challenge God's Word, you have an opening for the devil to come and attack. You've got to close up all the avenues and all the wonderments.... Get your mind not to wander, keep it channeled, keep it stayed upon God."[233]

> "Thou wilt keep him in perfect peace,
> whose mind is stayed on thee:
> because he trusteth in thee."[234]

This peace allows the Spirit of God to inspire us to be active in expressing what is true. This opens energy channels to the mouth and ears, protecting them from illnesses and infections. We are then able to hear and express truth on higher, more spiritual levels of understanding. Truth elevates our natural minds into spiritual ones. Our minds no longer focus on analyzations, wonderings, and fears but on what is true according to our faith in God. Trusting in Him provides us with a sense of peace.

God's Spirit is in the business of upholding the truth and exposing lies. This Spirit of truth is not recognized by people who do not share a genuine love for truth, especially about themselves. The *Aquarian Gospel* says, "I have many things to say unto you, but you cannot bear them now. Howbeit when she, the Spirit of Truth is come, she will guide you into all truth."[235] The Spirit of truth stands alone and will always honor the Word of God and urge us to separate ourselves from the deceitful hold of our ego.

Jesus Speaking the Truth to Deaf Ears

Jesus was an example of expressing truth to whoever He met. He dealt with the religious lies of the Pharisees by talking directly to their thoughts of error, which He called spirits. In this way, He shed light on them in order to give them a way out of their deceit. His bold approach was conveyed this way:

> "Ye are of your father the devil...
> He was a murderer from the beginning,
> and abode not in the truth,
> because there is no truth in him.
> When he speaketh a lie, he speaketh of his own:
> for he is a liar, and the father of it.
> And because I tell you the truth, ye believe me not.
> And if I say the truth, why do ye not believe me?
> He that is of God heareth God's words:
> ye therefore hear them not,
> because ye are not of God."[236]

When Jesus spoke, the Pharisees could not hear His words because their pride was offended. This is the first reaction of light hitting darkness. When pride begins its defense, you can know of a surety that it is defending a lie that has been perpetuated by error. It reacts in this defensive way because it is the motivating factor. A lie is not known as a lie by a liar. It is thought to be the truth; otherwise, it would not be believed. Error has some truth in it, which makes it believable. You can tell if a person is sent from God, for their message will always be convicting. They will tell the truth from God's perspective, despite the reactions they get from others. Truth gets a reaction within us so that we can see the error within us, for what it is.

Jesus knew that hearing His Father was the only voice of truth that was reliable. By hearing God and acting on that voice, He bore witness to what was true. It was void of self-motivation, human emotion, or self-justification. When He was rejected by those in authority, He was able to hold His own and not let the opinions of others sway Him. He conveyed this strength of character for our example, so that we might do it too. It only takes one voice to change the world. Consider yours important.

Hearing the Truth

> "We are of God: he that knoweth God heareth us;
> he that is not of God heareth not us.
> Hereby know we the spirit of truth,
> and the spirit of error."[237]

When the light of God's truth exposes error, negative reactions occur within us to divert our attention from the error that we are holding on to. Truth is meant to get this reaction so that we can see what is motivating us. If we can get past the reactions and maintain an open mind, truth can enter our hearts. This requires that we accept what may be hard to hear and resist the urge to deny it, for God wants us to change our attitude and selfish nature while we are here on earth.

Is our heart and mind open enough to hear objectively when anger clouds our judgment? Are we aware enough to see it when it is happening so that we can identify it? As hard as it can be to see it, truth spoken by someone at the right time can break open the shell of our darkness that would never be possible on our own. Next time we are in an argument with a loved one, we should consider that thought.

Our job is to keep the light on and work on those things that keep us in the dark in order to allow healing energies to flow freely to our mouth and ears. Vocalizing the truth about what we see in ourselves can separate us from the error of our ways. When we swear to our own hurt, we free ourselves from energy obstructions that would produce illness. Human nature continually seeks to battle with God's life in order to change His truth into a lie. Lies give us license to do whatever we want. We may think we can hide behind these lies we call truth, but everything we do is being recorded by the angels that accompany us. In effect, we are only lying to ourselves as we hide from what is true and real.

> "The heart is deceitful above all things,
> and desperately wicked:

who can know it?
I the LORD search the heart, I try the reins,
even to give every man according to his ways,
and according to the fruit of his doings."[238]

You are born into this life to know God by learning the truth and applying it. God hopes that you love Him enough to make it your own. His intent is for you to know Him and know Him well within yourself. But in order to do this, you must separate from the lies you believe so that the power of His life can become your own. You can be given all the directions of where to go, but until you drive the route yourself, you do not really know how to get there.

When we enter the spirit world, we will find that we will not be able to say one thing and mean something else, for we cannot lie there. All lies will be exposed. If we have not kept Jesus's commandments, we will not be comfortable there, for our inward nature has not been changed. If we are honest with God and true to ourselves now, we can form an eternal nature like God's while living in our natural body.

Bearing False Witness

We bear false witness when we are vocalizing false accusations that do not have their basis in the truth. Do we have a tendency to pass judgments without knowing the facts first? In Moses' day, truth was substantiated in the mouth of two or three witnesses:

"Never convict anyone on the testimony of one witness.
There must be at least two, and three is even better.
If anyone gives false witness,
claiming he has seen someone do wrong when he hasn't,
both men shall be brought
before the priests and judges....
They must be closely questioned,
and if the witness is lying,
his penalty shall be the punishment
he thought the other man would get.

> In this way you will purge out evil
> from among you."[239]

This is a divine law that happens automatically, slowly on earth and accelerated in the spiritual world. Our own judgments will always come back upon us to correct us. If we can identify our false accusations and refuse to cast the first stone, we will be better off. There are always two sides to every story. To spread the misinformation based on one side only is speculation and gossip.

Gossip

This is a common disease today to spread rumors that are accepted as fact. We can liken the behavior to mice that scurry to find the crumbs of destructive comments, which leave behind contagion and uncleanness. Gossip is done without resolving issues or conveying love for the person spoken about.

> "Take heed therefore how ye hear:
> for whosoever hath, to him shall be given;
> and whosoever hath not, from him shall be taken
> even that which he seemeth to have.
> For nothing is secret, that shall not be made
> manifest; neither any thing hid,
> that shall not be known and come abroad."[240]

Parts of information that we leave out creates an erroneous account that can hurt friends, family members, and coworkers.

> "Telling lies about someone is as harmful
> as hitting him with an axe,
> or wounding him with a sword,
> or shooting him with a sharp arrow."[241]

The following questions in the booklet *Tests of Character*[242] can help us pinpoint the unhealthy habit of gossip, which will give us an idea of whether we are prone to gossiping:

1. "Do I find it difficult to wait to tell someone when I have learned of a fault or sin committed by an acquaintance or neighbor or friend?"

2. "When I am in company, do I find myself quickly falling in with the conversation of others when its topic is the faults of others?"

If we said yes to either of these questions, there is a problem with gossiping. One way to rectify this is to give an honest, unembellished account of the facts, without painting a negative picture to others. Another way is to not voice anything at all and keep the person in prayer. A good point to remember is that what we see in others reminds us of what we do not like about ourselves.

Denial

Lying is a form of denial, a refusal to be honest with ourselves. This prevents us from taking responsibility for our actions and often results in hurting others. Facing the truth is one of the hardest things to do when dealing with denial, yet it is so freeing. Sometimes, we become hardened in our deceit, because we do not want to feel the pain of dealing with our emotions and weaknesses. Sometimes, we lie because we are afraid. When we continue down the road of denial, we empower the lies that we call truth. We evade responsibility in order to claim the role of a victim and blame others. Some people have lied so much that they can no longer recognize the truth.

Uncovering lies is a painful process, but addressing them is the only way to be healed. Truth forces us out into the light so that we can acknowledge our fears. Being honest about them is the first step to being real with ourselves. If we do not address them now, we will be compelled to do so after death. By that point, we will have solidified a nature of denial, which will make it difficult for us in the next life. The love for the truth about ourselves must be utilized now so that we can move on after death. The Word of God is provided to give us a way out now so that we can change.

"For the word of God is quick, and powerful,
and sharper than any two-edged sword,

piercing even to the dividing asunder of soul and spirit,
and of the joints and marrow, and is a discerner
of the thoughts and intents of the heart.
Neither is there any creature
that is not manifest in his sight:
but all things are naked and opened unto the eyes
of him with whom we have to do."[243]

When we cannot be true to ourselves, we cannot be true to God or others. We have to keep our word to ourselves in order to be trusted by another person. As it says in *Anatomy of the Spirit,* "Genuine, complete healing requires honesty with oneself. An inability to be honest obstructs healing as seriously as the inability to forgive. Honesty and forgiveness retrieve our energy—our spirits—from the energy dimension of 'the past.'"[244] If we are serious about healing, we must make decisions that we stick to at our own expense. True love for ourselves requires principle and discipline.

There are two very good books on honesty and self-deceit if you would like to study this more in depth: *The Lies We Believe,* by Dr. Chris Thurman, and *People of the Lie,* by M. Scott Peck. Both books shed light on the psychology of human nature and how to uncover and address self-lies.

Spiritual Correspondence of the Ears

Hearing the truth and the still small voice of God is the spiritual purpose of our ears. Applying what we hear from God maintains a spiritual balance in our lives that is necessary for the greatest energy flow to our ears. In the highest heavens, truth that is heard by the angels is immediately implemented into life. This constitutes life in the celestial heavens, where hearing and doing are one. Truth that is heard and thought about first, before being implemented, constitutes life among the spiritual angels. The more we listen and implement what is true and good, the deeper our connection will be with the angels of that realm.

Spiritual Causes of Hearing Problems

Problems with the ears occur because of what we are listening to or what we refuse to listen to. Listening to erroneous ideas and gossip, or refusing to hear the truth about ourselves, can produce hearing problems. If our eardrums are damaged, our balance can become affected. This corresponds to listening to wrong ideas, which create instability in our walk of life. If we have hearing problems from birth, the spiritual cause is produced from the behaviors from those in our hereditary line who had strong habits of rejecting truth.

Refusing these tendencies in our own lives draws angelic forces to us to assist in our healing. Once we have made a habit of identifying these causes in our lives, we have set in motion spiritual healing.

If our working environment has created hearing loss, wisdom would dictate that we do something to eliminate our exposure to it. If circumstances are beyond our control, and we unknowingly suffered hearing loss, we should not condemn ourselves or find fault with God, who has allowed it. Nothing can come to us without a divine plan and purpose. We may be reaping for periods in our lives when we refused to listen to God by following through on the impressions that we were given. We can lovingly make a point to have an entreatable ear toward a loving Man, who is always showing us new ways to free ourselves. Finding the joy in this will help us be softer and pliable to His divine voice. When we are doing our best to implement the messages God is giving us, we strengthen our inner hearing. This will produce freedom from these hereditary influences after death.

Spiritual Causes and Antidotes for Itching Ears

One reason why our ears itch is that we are listening to things that are not good or true. This is usually because of lies that we believe. We are not aware that these are lies at the time, but we can consider them convenient truths: lies that we want to be our truth.

I had itching ears during a time of great duress and failed to identify the spiritual cause. After a time, I realized I was not listening to what was good or true. Once I recognized the correlation to my condition,

I saw the necessity of hearing what I did not want to. I addressed this negative desire as a spirit, cast it out in Jesus's name, and replaced it with an entreatable angel. The itching disappeared.

"God is present with us to the degree
that we love goodness and truth."[245]

Willingness to listen to anything from anyone can only help us be a better person. Others may say it wrong, but there is truth there. If there is someone we do not want to listen to, we should pay them greater heed, for it will only develop our character. Listening to the truth from our enemy will help us be wise as a serpent, but harmless as a dove.

When our heart turns away from wanting to hear the truth, we draw to ourselves teachers and acquaintances that are of like disposition to confirm the falsities that we are calling our truth. Unless we have light from the Word of God to expose the error, we can easily succumb to lies: personal ones, social ones, religious ones, or lies accepted by our generation.

"For the time will come
when they will not endure sound doctrine;
but after their own lusts shall they heap to themselves
teachers, having itching ears;
And they shall turn away their ears from the truth,
and shall be turned unto fables."[246]

Sadly, this is the present state of our generation. For the love of truth has been changed into a desire for lies. This also permeates the religious world, producing many teachers who no longer present the truth that Jesus's commandments must be lived in order to enter heaven. Jesus's death is used as an excuse that He did it all without any responsibility on our part. This discredits His words and His life, as we see in the book of 1 John:

"He that saith, I know him,
and keepeth not his commandments,

is a liar, and the truth is not in him.
But whoso keepeth his word,
in him verily is the love of God perfected:
hereby know we that we are in him.
He that saith he abideth in him
ought himself also so to walk, even as he walked."[247]

Spiritual Causes of Ear Infections

Ear infections are painful and reflect more anger or rage at being told something that we do not want to hear. Inflammation corresponds to inner anger and stress. Rejecting advice reveals an unwillingness to change our present behavior. The anger is utilized as a smoke screen to prevent us from hearing or doing what is right.

Children under the age of accountability who get ear infections are reflecting the anger of their parents. Parents can then make an application for themselves by identifying their refusal to listen, casting it out of their life through prayer, and replacing it with entreatableness. This will assist in their child's healing. I have witnessed this many times in my life with my children and other children. Once the parents get the message, the child's healing begins.

Parents can be an example at home of the behavior that they want their children to emulate. Children are keen at watching and copying the behaviors of parents and friends. If we are honest with ourselves and correct our behavior in their presence, they will learn from it. Surrounding them with positive examples will help them understand the importance of listening.

Learning to be entreatable to God's voice is a day-to-day leading that requires us to be spontaneous and open to change. This way, we learn how to let God lead us, and our children will follow our example.

Antidotes for Ear Infections

"A fool hates his father's instruction, but a wise son puts it into practice."[248]

"And you must think constantly about these commandments I am giving you today. You must teach them to your children and talk about them when you are at home or out for a walk; at bedtime and the first thing in the morning."[249]

"Poverty and shame is waiting for those who refuse instruction, but he who accepts criticism will be honored. It is nice to see things come together, but fools refuse to change even when they see it is wrong. You become wiser by associating with wise men."[250]

Spiritual Causes of Mouth Problems

The mouth is the vehicle that we use to express the truth or deny it. Problems in the mouth area convey a deficiency in the expression of truth in our life. Laryngitis, strep throat, or problems with the jaw are caused by speaking evil about someone, gossiping, or refusing to defend what is true or good. When we inadvertently bite our tongue, it reveals that hurtful criticisms and biting responses are present. Clenching of teeth reveals an anger that wants its way and can't let go. Its strong will locks the jaw because loving expressions have been thwarted.

Antidotes for Mouth Problems

Below are some scriptural antidotes that when applied will assist in healing the mouth and throat:

"A fool utters slanderous remarks. A person who talks too much ends up putting his foot in his mouth, but a wise person makes every word count. People will listen to a wise man because his words mean something. No one pays attention to the person who talks too much."[251]

"A gossiper tells everything he knows so do not tell him anything you don't want repeated."[252]

"A foolish man speaks with pride but the righteous man weighs what he says before he speaks."[253]

"A stupid man holds a grudge and hates his neighbor, but a wise man waits before making a decision. A gossip tells things that should not be said, but a trustworthy man is silent."[254]

"A truthful man is known by his honesty in the same way a liar is known by his deceitfulness. Some people's words hurt like being stabbed with a knife, but the words of the wise are soothing and healthful. Truth will stand forever, but lies are soon found out. Those who plot evil have deceitful hearts, but joy and peace are in the hearts of them who plan good. Nothing bad happens to those who are good, but the evil have constant problems. The Lord hates a liar but delights in those who are truthful. A wise man hides his intelligence, but the fool broadcasts his idiocy."[255]

"Do not pass along untrue reports. Do not cooperate with an evil man by affirming on the witness stand something you know is false. Don't join mobs intent on evil. When on the witness stand, don't be swayed in your testimony by the mood of the majority present, and do not slant your testimony in favor of a man just because he is poor."[256]

"Liars are caught in their own lies. The just are saved by their truthfulness. Truthfulness and hard work bring a man great satisfaction. A fool never listens to advice, but the wise man always listens. A fool cannot hold his temper and it shows, while the prudent man never shows it in public."[257]

"You must not ... lie nor defraud. You must not swear to a falsehood.... Don't gossip. Don't falsely accuse your neighbor of some crime, for I am Jehovah. Don't hate your brother. Rebuke anyone who sins; don't let him get away with it, or you will be equally guilty."[258]

"Lord, who may go and find refuge and shelter in your tabernacle up on your holy hill? Anyone who leads a blameless life and is truly sincere. Anyone who refuses to slander others, does not listen to gossip … speaks out against sin, criticizes those committing it, commends the faithful followers of the Lord, keeps a promise even if it ruins him … and refuses to testify against the innocent despite the bribes offered him—such a man shall stand firm forever."[259]

"To quarrel with a neighbor is foolish; a man with good sense holds his tongue. A gossip goes around spreading rumors, while a trustworthy man tries to quiet them."[260]

"Stop lying to each other; tell the truth, for we are parts of each other and when we lie to each other we are hurting ourselves."[261]

"Swear not at all."[262]

"Say just a simple, 'Yes, I will' or 'No, I won't.' Your word is enough. To strengthen your promise with a vow shows that something is wrong."[263]

"So when you talk to God and vow to him that you will do something, don't delay in doing it, for God has no pleasure in fools. Keep your promise to him. It is far better not to say you'll do something than to say you will and then not do it."[264]

Thou Shalt Not Covet
Eyes and Lungs
Contentment, Temperance, and Joy

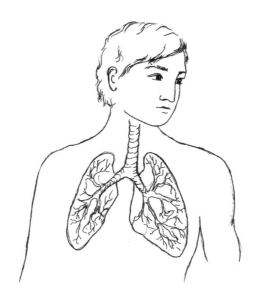

The Tenth Commandment
Figure 13

Chapter 12

The Tenth Commandment

"Thou shalt not covet thy neighbor's house,
thou shalt not covet thy neighbor's wife, nor his
manservant, nor his maidservant, nor his ox, nor his
ass, nor any thing that is thy neighbor's."
Exodus 20:17; Deuteronomy 5:21

Coveting is an excessive desire to obtain the possessions of others. This desire can become all-consuming and blind us to think that it is right. The obsessive interest can become an addiction, a selfish passion that leads us to pursue it for personal conquest. It can cause us to lie, cheat, or steal with all manner of justification in order to obtain what is not rightfully ours to have.

The act of coveting affects the health of our eyes and lungs. The eyes eagerly widen at the sight of the wanted possessions in order to take another's belongings. The inspiration causes our breathing to become short and shallow, as tension increases to obtain it. This produces a weakening in our forcefields governing the lungs and eyes. Over time, deficiencies will begin to manifest in these areas of the body.

The Breath of Life

When God created man, He created within him everything that he needed to have in order to live in love and communication with Him. He breathed into Adam's nostrils the breath of life, enabling him to become a living soul (Genesis 2:7). The word "breath," in this context in the Hebrew, means divine inspiration. As we breathe in, we are taking in God's life, which by representation is His inspiration. This gives us guidance and direction in life and keeps us alive and connected to the heavens. It was God's intent that Adam live by this inspiration in order to remain in communication with His thoughts and feelings.

> "But there is a spirit in man:
> and the inspiration of the Almighty
> giveth them understanding."[265]

Divine Inspiration

Divine inspiration not only enhances the flow of energy to our lungs, it also provides us with understanding and fills our mind's eye with light. Jesus said that when our eye is single on what is true, our whole body will be filled with light. This light can radiate from the eyes and face of a person who is being led by it. Some can see this light with spiritual eyes. In scripture, we see this actualized in Moses, who after receiving the second set of Ten Commandments, radiated a light from his face so bright that when the people saw it, they were afraid. As a result, he put a veil over his face.

When we understand the truth and apply it, it produces an energizing light from our face, for our mind has become enlightened. When we follow the truth to be useful with what we know, the forcefields around our eyes and face are empowered. This is because we are perceiving truth from the light of heaven and not from our own understanding.

The Lungs

The purpose of our lungs is to take in oxygen from the air and remove carbon dioxide as waste. According to *The Human Body Book*, "Air enters the lungs from the trachea which branches at its base into two main airways, the primary bronchi.... The primary bronchus divides into secondary bronchi, and these subdivide into tertiary bronchi.... This intricate network of air passages resembles an inverted tree, with the trachea as the trunk, and is known as the bronchial tree."[266] The branches of this tree bring oxygen into our body. If you look at the picture of the lungs in Figure 13 upside down, you can see this picture of the tree.

It is interesting to note that the wisdom of God in scripture is referred to as a tree of life. The upside-down tree that has been planted within us is a shadow or type of this truth. Hidden in this tree of life is the wisdom and inspiration from the Creator that lies within us. Following leadings and impressions from God helps maintain the health of our lungs.

> "Happy is the man that findeth wisdom....
> She is a tree of life to them that lay hold upon her:
> and happy is every one that retaineth her."[267]

The condition of our lungs is determined not only by preventative health measures, but by how well we follow the inspiration of wisdom that comes from the Holy Spirit. This Spirit inspires us with thoughts and actions of self-denial so that we can address the desires of covetousness within ourselves. When we follow them, we are filled with an inward contentment and joy. By complying with our first thoughts and feelings, we are able to overcome our selfish tendencies. Denying ourselves takes practice and sacrifice. When we do, we receive greater inspiration from the love of God. This love empowers our God-given nature. It is life-giving and speaks to our heart, bringing to our remembrance words from God that nourish our souls and spirits.

Breathing Fully Lowers Anxiety Levels

Breathing slowly and fully helps regulate our anxiety levels. When we relax and breathe in, our lungs expand. The increased oxygen and blood flow recharges our body and refreshes our attitude. Clean air in forests and in mountainous areas invigorates our minds, heals our bodies, and gives us a fresh, new perspective.

When we are fearful or are under stress, we need to learn how to breathe. Stress normally causes us to breathe in a more shallow way. To counteract this anxiety, we can purposely breathe in a fuller and slower way to disengage our emotions and shift mental gears. Relaxing under pressure allows us take a step back and face stressful situations with more composure and energy. When we make a practice of breathing this way, we balance our mind and spirit and keep headaches at bay, for this increases airflow to our brains.

Unconscious thinking patterns can actually control our breathing. If we notice that we are breathing shallow, we should take a moment and examine our thoughts and feelings. We can address the tension by changing the way we are reacting and the way we are breathing. This, in turn, will affect our thinking pattern and allow us to respond in a more relaxed state. In this way, we maintain a higher awareness and are more open to hearing and receiving God's inspirations and thoughts.

Laughter

Laughter is another way to increase our airflow. It can also be utilized as an anesthetic to pain. In Norman Cousins's book, *Anatomy of an Illness,* ten minutes of genuine belly laughter provided him with two hours of pain-free sleep as he struggled with a connective tissue disorder. He upped his vitamin C levels, watched funny movies, and had humorous books read to him in order to help boost his immune system. He stated in his book, "Hearty laughter is a good way to jog internally without having to go outdoors."[268]

Laughter is a great antidote when physical conditions keep us housebound. A sunny, positive attitude boosts our immune systems. Take time for yourself during the day. Surround yourself with beauty and the things that you love. If you want to tickle your fancy and bring some cheer to your life, read *Dave Barry's Only Travel Guide You'll Ever Need* or watch Jim Gaffigan, the funny comedian on Netflix. Keeping your spirits up will help rejuvenate your mind and your body. Being happy produces healing. ☺

Respiratory Disorders

There are many respiratory disorders that affect the lungs, causing restriction to our airflow. Some of these are bronchitis, pneumonia, emphysema, asthma, and tuberculosis. *The Human Body Book* gives a description for each of them: "Bronchitis is inflammation of the bronchi, which are the larger airways that branch from the base of the trachea, or windpipe, into the lungs." Pneumonia is "inflammation of the lung's microscopic air sacs, which line the lung and the smaller airways, the bronchioles." In emphysema, "the air sacs (alveoli) become overstretched.... As a result, the lungs overinflate, the volume of air moving in and out of the lungs is reduced, and less oxygen is absorbed into the bloodstream." Asthma is "an inflammatory lung disease that causes recurrent attacks of breathlessness and wheezing due to the narrowed airways in the lungs." Tuberculosis, an "infectious disease, mainly affecting the lung tissue, is caused by the bacterium mycobacterium tuberculosis." [269]

Spiritual Causes of Respiratory Disorders

Below is a list of respiratory disorders along with their corresponding spiritual causes:

According to *God Can Heal You,* the following are the spiritual causes for respiratory disorders. Understanding these causes will help us uncover our antidotes.

- "Bronchitis: Not easy to be entreated; insensitivity to the Spirit of God."
- "Pneumonia: Overwhelmed by evil emotions; lack of trust in God in very trying situations; very cold to God."
- "Emphysema: Resisting the Holy Ghost; stubbornness; inflexibility; great restriction in allowing the Holy Spirit to inspire."
- "Asthma: Not trusting in God; proud; very haughty spiritually."
- "Respiratory tuberculosis: Spiritual filthiness; uncleanness; stagnation of spirit; lacking the fear of God; disobedience to God's Spirit." [270]

All respiratory disorders have to do with how we are reacting to the leadings and impressions that come from God.

Once we identify these causes in our lives, we can counteract the negative behavior by acting in the opposite manner. If it is pride motivating us, act in humble ways. If it is insensitivity, look for ways to be more entreatable to God's inspirations. If it is stubbornness, practice being open-minded to others. The real antidote is in the action we take, for this will assist in healing the affected areas.

"Keep a close watch on all you do and think.
Stay true to what is right and
God will bless you and use you to help others."[271]

Antidotes for Respiratory Disorders

"Wherefore do ye spend money for that which is not bread? and your labour for that which satisfieth not? hearken diligently unto me, and eat ye that which is good, and let your soul delight itself in fatness."[272]

"Let your conversation be without covetousness; and be content with such things as ye have: for he hath said, I will never leave thee, nor forsake thee."[273]

"Let there be no ... impurity or greed among you. Let no one be able to accuse you of any such things.... You can be sure of this: The kingdom of Christ and of God will never belong to anyone who is impure or greedy, for a greedy person is really an idol worshipper—he loves and worships the good things of this life more than God."[274]

"Tell those who are rich not to be proud and not to trust in their money, which will soon be gone, but their pride and trust should be in the living God who always richly gives us all we need for our enjoyment. Tell them to use their money to do good. They should be rich in good works and should give happily to those in need, always being ready to share with others whatever God has given them. By doing this they will be storing up real treasure for themselves in heaven—it is the only safe investment for eternity! And they will be living a fruitful Christian life down here as well."[275]

Choking and the Spiritual Causes

"And these are they which are sown among thorns;
such as hear the word, and the cares of this world,
and the deceitfulness of riches,
and the lusts of other things entering in,
choke the word, and it becometh unfruitful."[276]

This scripture contains three pursuits that cause the Word of God to be "choked" in our lives: the cares of the world, undue importance on money, and excessive desires for other things. The truth cannot take root when these take priority in a life. If we have a bout of choking or coughing, we have to ask ourselves, what am I thinking or feeling that is restricting God's inspiration in my life right now? It may be what we were thinking about or talking about at that moment.

Excessive phlegm is produced when we have been overcome with proud motivations and desires. As a result, we do things in excess because of pride or its reactions of anger. When these are not identified in our lives, excess phlegm begins to manifest itself.

Once we identify the cause, simply cast it out and replace it with the opposite: positive angelic qualities. Look for ways to implement new behavior. Another simple way of casting out spirits is to say the word "peace." This mitigates the affecting spiritual influences within and around us and clears the air in spirit. This is a command that Jesus gave us to say whenever entering into a house. We can do the same when we need to make a change in our spiritual state. I have found it very beneficial to use and have witnessed my day go much better when using it.

"And into whatsoever house, ye enter, first say,
Peace, be to this house."[277]

The Deceitfulness of Riches

Sometimes, we are unaware that the desire for money and the acquiring of possessions are the very things that prevent us from being useful to God. The more one acquires, the more time and money are needed for their upkeep. Priorities shift, and we become unaware that we are being robbed from pursuing what is more important in life.

Below is a story that reveals the end result of a life consumed by material wealth and the selfish use of it:

The Rich Man and Lazarus

Jesus told this story about a rich man and Lazarus in Luke 16:19–31, which I have paraphrased below:

A diseased beggar named Lazarus, who was full of sores, would often lay at a rich man's door to eat the scraps from his table. The rich man had everything he wanted, and his life consisted of many possessions, but the diseased beggar was a righteous man who was in need.

After both men died, the beggar was carried by the angels to a place where the righteous went near Abraham, but the soul of the rich man was tormented by the fire of his unregulated passions. He had lived luxuriously and selfishly while on earth. He asked Abraham to send Lazarus to him to cool his tongue, since he was in such anguish.

Abraham reminded him that during his lifetime, he had everything he wanted, and Lazarus had nothing. Now he was comforted, and there was a great gulf between the two men so that neither could cross over to the other side.

The rich man begged Abraham to send Lazarus to his home to warn his five brothers of a similar plight. Their lifestyles had been the same as his, and he knew this place of torment existed for them as well. Abraham refused, telling the rich man that they had the scriptures to help them.

The rich man replied that they would not bother to read them, but they would listen if someone returned from the dead. Abraham told him that if they would not listen to the scriptures, they would not change, even if someone from the dead came back to warn them. In reality, their internal nature would have to change by personally applying these scriptures for themselves. No one outside of them could do this for them. A man who appeared from the dead could not make that happen.

Life after death continues with what we have loved the most. In this case, the rich man's selfish desire for luxury created his place of torment. We create the place that we go to after death by the decisions that we make, for they have solidified our nature. The rich man was given the opportunity to change his life by being given access to the Word of God. This would have informed him how to put the selfish life last, but he chose to indulge himself instead. The beggar made the right choice by loving the truth, but he was poor and ill. His reward and comfort was a heavenly life. Passion for material wealth must be disciplined with a love for truth in order for a person to gain entrance into heaven.

> "For what shall it profit a man,
> if he shall gain the whole world, and lose his own soul?
> Or what shall a man give in exchange for his soul?"[278]

The Lusts of Other Things: Compulsive Buying and Excessive Possessions

Some people are compulsive buyers, having ten pairs of shoes and excessive amounts of items. Indulgence leads to hoarding and overspending, usually for emotional security. Some hoarders surround themselves with unused and unneeded possessions because of fear and will not let go of them.

There was an instance in our town where a woman had so much stuff in her house that the floors of her home eventually collapsed from the weight of it all, and she died there. This is a sad yet extreme example, but one that teaches a very valuable lesson.

> "Take heed, and beware of covetousness:
> for a man's life consisteth not in
> the abundance of the things
> which he possesseth."[279]

When obtaining possessions confiscate the simple joys that life has to offer, we are taken over by a false drive that makes us feel discontent. This drive seeks to fulfill itself by obtaining things wrongfully. It says in the book, *Breaking the Habit of Being Yourself,* "If we wait for anything outside us to make us happy, then we are not following the quantum law. We are relying on the outer to change the inner…. We have to become happy *before* our abundance shows up."[280] Living contently in a world run by money is a pearl of great price that we must strive for.

"But godliness with contentment is great gain."[281]

"After all, we didn't bring any money with us
when we came into the world,
and we can't carry away a single penny when we die.
So we should be well satisfied without money
if we have enough food and clothing.
But people who long to be rich
soon begin to do all kinds of wrong things
to get money, things that hurt them
and make them evil-minded and
finally send them to hell itself.
For the love of money
is the first step toward all kinds of sin.
Some people have even turned away from God
because of their love for it,
and as a result have pierced themselves
with many sorrows."[282]

Recognizing Darkness with Spiritual Eyes

Truth provides light to our spiritual eyes so that we can identify what may be unlike God within ourselves. God's desire is that we see these things from an elevated perspective so that we can turn away from them. If we do not turn away from what we know is unlike God within ourselves, we will be unable to recognize what is truly good because our understanding will be darkened. According to *Heaven and Hell,* translated by George Dole, "We are born into evils of all kinds, evils which need to be taken away if we are to be saved. They cannot be taken away unless we see them within ourselves, admit that they are there, then refuse them and ultimately turn away from them. Only then are they taken away. This cannot happen unless we are exposed to both good and evil, since it is from good that we can see evils, though we cannot see what is good from evil."[283] This helps us understand the need to identify good and evil from the perspective of truth and not from our own opinions. Our choices in how we perceive things will either unveil or veil us.

Spiritual Causes of Eye Problems

Visual impairments reveal a false perception of truth, an unwillingness to see ourselves, or calling good evil and evil good. Eye problems also reveal excessive wants and desires. In all of these cases, we remain unaware because our perception has become blinded by what we love.

Antidotes for Eye Problems: Our Perception

We can turn off stress to our mind and body by changing our perspective. How we perceive a thing determines our emotional state. When we correct the way we look at something, our attitude will change as well.

I have learned in my personal life that negative reactions are often inspired by a wrong perception. Situations get blown out of proportion because expectations are too high, and pride is dominating my reasoning. These reactions become my truth, whether they are true or not. For example, if I am facing an overwhelming task, I catch myself when I hear the overwhelmed voice in my mind saying, "Oh, my God!" Believing the negative reaction causes me to function in an overwhelmed state of mind. When I catch myself believing the lie of it, I tell myself the opposite: "This is no big deal." I find out that by doing the task with this mind-set, it is actually easier than my initial reaction made it seem. My negative perspective had made the job harder. Every situation holds valuable opportunities to find more ways to become spiritual and elevate our understanding. Then we can live in a more contented and trusting state of mind, knowing that everything happens for our good.

Contentment, Temperance, and Joy

Being content provides us with temperance, which gives us a balanced perspective. We can see clearly with less stress and are more open to new inspirations from God to make us better. Living this way not only prevents lung and eye problems, it also rejuvenates our spiritual body. True joy comes from being useful with the thoughts and ideas that God gives to us daily.

Our natural mind always desires more than is needed, but when we operate with a spiritual mind, we live more simply and desire less. Trusting in God allows us to let go of possessions. The closer we get to God, our material possessions take on less meaning. This is because our true essence is not natural but spiritual.

> "I have learned, in whatsoever state I am,
> therewith to be content.
> I know both how to be abased, and
> I know how to abound: every where and in all things
> I am instructed both to be full and to be hungry,
> both to abound and to suffer need.
> I can do all things through Christ
> which strengtheneth me."[284]

Conclusion

Faith in God's Word that is motivated by love is the key to unlocking the mysteries of healing. This allows the power of God to take effect in our lives. By realigning our lives with the antidotes from the scriptures, the life of God is freed and activated within us. This make us whole in body and mind.

God allowed Himself to be put in a position that is common to man by visiting us. The struggle was to remain faithful to God, look like a sinner to many, and to maintain His usefulness to God. He did so under great duress, and He did it alone. He never stopped revealing spirits that were unlike God in everyone around Him, even at His own expense, leaving Him without the needed help. He was able to keep the light of God's work alive while being devastated by it.

This should provide us with a sense of hope, that if He can do it, we can do it too, no matter what hardships life brings us through, no matter what illnesses we face, and whether we are healed or not. God always provides a light of hope. He will always look at the heart and does not define us by what we go through, but by how we take it. This is the hope for us and a generation that has come to the end of its age. God has a divine purpose and plan for allowing the illnesses that we experience and has our eternal good in mind.

I am grateful for the opportunity to share these thoughts and inspirations with you. I may have never met you, but I hope these antidotes will bring you closer to God through their daily application. In doing so, they will heal your spirit and prepare you for a heavenly life.

If you enjoyed this book, please share your thoughts on my Facebook page, Antidotes for Healing the Human Body. If you know of a friend, a loved one, or a business colleague who is ill or in need of spiritual insight and healing, I hope you will share this book and my website: www.antidotesforhealing.com. with them. This site contains a section called "Antidotes," which provides a library of illnesses with their spiritual causes and antidotes. This can be used as a quick reference for health problems as they occur. May God bless you in your endeavor toward healing.

The Ten Commandments of Life

Because

I. I (God) AM Life

There is only One True Way to:

II. Express Life
III. Receive Life
IV. Respect Life
V. Preserve Life
VI. Live Life
VII. Love Life
VIII. Give Life
IX. Present Life
X. Recognize Life

The Ten Commandments and Their Application for Health

The Commandment and Body Part	Comment	Jesus' Words	Application	Quality	Diseases
Love God First Ex 20:1-3 **The Blood** Le 17:11-14	That which one loves above all else is his god: ie. achievement, wealth, reputation.	Love the Lord thy God with all thy heart, and with all thy soul, and with all thy mind. Matthew 22:37	If a man think himself to be something when he is nothing, he deceiveth himself. Galatians 6:3	Every Whit Whole	Blood Diseases and Problems
No Images Ex 20:4-6 **Heart, Senses, and Mind**	Loving a false image that self produces	No man can serve two masters. Matthew 6:24	If any man love the world, the love of the Father is not in him. 1 John 2:15b	Sanity, Intelligence, Stability	Heart Problems and Mental Instability
Taking the Lord's Name in Vain Ex 20:7 **Mouth, Throat, and Teeth**	Profaning, rejecting or despising the truth about God or oneself	Every idle word that men shall speak, they shall give account. Matthew 12:36	Who is a wise man? Let him show out of a good conversation his works with meekness of wisdom. James 3:13	Manners Good Speech	Mouth, Throat and Tooth Problems
Keep the Sabbath Day Ex 20:8-11 **Nervous System**	Being led by God in daily life brings peace and restfulness to the inner man.	The sabbath was made for man and not man for the sabbath. Mark 2:27	Peace I leave with you… Let not your heart be troubled, neither let it be afraid. John 14:27a, c	Good Memory, Mediator, Calm	Insomnia, Restless Legs, Alzheimer's, Parkinson's Diseases
Honor Parents Ex 20:12 **Muscles, Ligaments, and Sinew**	A mother and father are God's image and likeness (Genesis 1:27)	For whosoever shall do the will of my Father…the same is my brother, and sister, and mother. Matthew 12:50a, c	Obey them that have rule over you, and submit yourselves. Hebrews 13:17a	Obedience	Muscle Problems

Figure 14

The Commandment and Body Part	Comment	Jesus' Words	Application	Quality	Diseases
No Murder Ex 20:13 **Liver, Gall Bladder, Spleen, and Skin**	One must not hate his brother or neighbor, or defame or slander him from hatred, cruelty, or revenge.	Love ye your enemies, and do good...and your reward shall be great. Forgive and ye shall be forgiven Luke 6:35-37	Thou shalt not avenge, nor bear any grudge... thou shalt love thy neighbor as thyself. Leviticus 19:18	Love, Long-suffering, Forgiveness	Liver Diseases, Gallstones, Cancer, and Skin Irritations
No Adultery Ex 20:14 **Reproductive Organs**	The love of marriage is love for God.	Whosoever looketh on a woman to lust after her hath committed adultery with her already in his heart. Matthew 5:28	Whoso committeth adultery...lacketh understanding: he that doeth it destroyeth his own soul. Proverbs 6:32	Faithful	Infertility, Miscarriages, Uterine Fibroids, Venereal diseases
No Stealing Ex 20:15 **Hands, Feet, and Eyes**	Open theft, unlawful usury or gain, bribery, overcharging	The thief cometh not, but for to steal, and to kill, and to destroy: I am come that they might have life. John 10:10	Let him that stole steal no more: but rather let him labor, working with his hands the thing which is good. Ephesians 4:28	Generous and Good	Eye, Hand and Foot Problems
No False Witness Ex 20:16 **Ears and Mouth**	Lying and accusing falsely	For this cause came I into the world, that I should bear witness unto the truth. John 18:37b	Swear not at all.."Say just a simple, Yes I will', or 'No I won't.' To strengthen your word with a vow shows something is wrong." Matthew 5:34a, 37LB	Truthful	Ear and Mouth Problems
No Coveting Ex 20:17 **Eyes and Lungs**	Excessive desire to obtain another's possessions and wealth	What shall it profit a man, if he gain the whole world, and loose his own soul? Mark 8:36-37	For the love of money is the root of all evil. 1 Timothy 6:10a	Contented, Temperate and Joyful	Respiratory Disorders and Eye Problems

Figure 15

"When man has reached the place
where he has faith in God,
in nature and himself,
he knows the Word of power;
his word is balm for every wound,
is cure for all the ills of life.
The healer is the man
who can inspire faith.
The tongue may speak to human ears,
but souls are reached
by souls that speak to souls."

Jesus [285]

Notes

Notes

Notes

Notes

Notes

End Notes

1   Proverbs 23:7.

2   John 3:27b.

3   John 5:14b.

4   Mark 10:52b.

5   Proverbs 14:12.

6   Psalm 91:9–11.

7   John 8:31b, 32.

8   Jeremiah 6:16b, 19.

9   James 2:24.

10   Matthew 19:17b.

11   1 John 2:4.

12   Exodus 15:26.

13   Psalm 19:1–3.

14   Romans 1:20.

15   1 Corinthians 2:14, 15a, 16b *The Living Bible*. Carol Stream, IL: Tyndale House Publishers, Inc. 1971.

16   Norman Vincent Peale. *The Power of Positive Thinking*. New York: FIRESIDE, a division of Simon & Schuster, Inc. 2008, 143.

17   Isaiah 46:9b.

18   Luke 18:18b, 19.

19   John 5:44.

20   Matthew 23:9–12.

21   Matthew 23:7–8, 11 TLB.

22   John 7:18.

23   John 17:3.

24   Romans 8:6–7.

25   John 6:53.

26   John 6:57.

27 Steve Parker. *The Human Body Book.* New York: DK Publishing, Penguin Random House, 2007, 116, 126.

28 Genesis 4:10b.

29 Proverbs 8:33, 35–36.

30 John 15: 3, 7.

31 Deuteronomy 30:19–20a.

32 Luke 14:26.

33 Matthew 6:24, 33.

34 Dr. Joe Dispenza. *Breaking the Habit of Being Yourself.* Carlsbad, CA: Hay House, 2012, 78–79.

35 Daniel 3:17b–18.

36 Job 13:15a.

37 James 1:2b–5a, 6–8 TLB.

38 Revelation 22:9b.

39 Emanuel Swedenborg. *Heaven and Hell.* New York: Swedenborg Foundation, 1978, 123 n. 230.

40 Proverbs 18:24b.

41 Psalm 4:4b.

42 John 14:27a, c.

43 Psalm 27:14.

44 Psalm 61:2b.

45 Ezekiel 36:25b–27.

46 Proverbs 17:22a.

47 Parker, *The Human Body Book*, 127.

48 Matthew 22:37b–39.

49 James 1:8.

50 1 Samuel 15:22–23.

51 Caroline Myss. *Anatomy of the Spirit.* New York: MJF Books/Penguin Random House, 1996, 229–230.

52 1 John 4:18a.

53 2 Timothy 1:7.

54 James 3:17–18.

55 Isaiah 26:3.

56 Romans 12:2.

57 Isaiah 55:9b.

58 Exodus 4:11b, d, 12.

59 James 1:26 TLB.

60 Proverbs 18:21.

61 Isaiah 29:13b.

62 Job 6:24.

63 Proverbs 12:18b.

64 Proverbs 12:14–19 TLB.

65 Proverbs 10:19–20 TLB.

66 Proverbs 10: 21.

67 Psalm 34:12–14 TLB.

68 Ecclesiastes 5:2.

69 Colossians 4:6.

70 John Worcester. *Physiological Correspondences.* Bryn Athyn, PA: Swedenborg Scientific Association, 1987, 223.

71 Proverbs 25:19.

72 Daniel 12:4b.

73 Matthew 11:28–30.

74 Isaiah 58:6–8a.

75 Etienne de Grellet du Mabillier.

76 Hebrews 4:1–2, 10–11.

77 Luke 9:24.

78 Parker, *The Human Body Book,* 68.

79 James 1:4.

80 Psalm 127:1a, 2b.

81 Matthew 6:34 TLB.

82 Job 33:14–17.

83 Proverbs 4:26–27.

84 Jeremiah 6:16b.

85 Joshua 1:3a, 7.

86 Micah 6:8.

87 *God Can Heal You.* New Britain, CT: Truth Center, Inc., 1987, 5.

88 Proverbs 4:4b–6.

89 James 1:25.

90 Deuteronomy 8:11, 17, 18a, 19a, c.

91 John 14:26.

92 Charles B. Clayman. *The Human Body.* New York: DK Publishing/Penguin Random House, 1995, 81.

93 Clayman, *The Human Body,* 81.

94 *God Can Heal You,* 5.

95 Louise Hay. *You Can Heal Your Life.* Carlsbad, CA: Hay House Inc., 2004, 191.

96 Henry Wright. *A More Excellent Way to Be In Health.* New Kensington, PA: Whitaker House, 2009, 259.

97 Psalm 131:2.

98 Proverbs 16:3.

99 Isaiah 49:15.

100 Psalm 68:5a.

101 Psalm 27:10.

102 Matthew 23:9.

103 Mark 3:33b, 35.

104 Hebrews 5:8

105 Romans 8:14.

106 Proverbs 3:1b–8 TLB.

107 Deuteronomy 30:15, 19b–20a TLB.

108 Matthew 6:7–8 TLB.

109 Proverbs 1:5, 7–9.

110 Proverbs 3:11–12.

111 Ephesians 6:1–4 TLB.

112 Hebrews 13:17a.

113 Isaiah 48:4b.

114 Jeremiah 17:23.

115 Deuteronomy 31:27a, c.

116 Deuteronomy 10:12b–13 TLB.

117 Deuteronomy 10:16 TLB.

118 Psalm 75:5b.

119 Proverbs 1:23.

120 Genesis 4:9b.

121 Levi Dowling. Reprinted from *The Aquarian Gospel of Jesus the Christ*. DeVorss Publications 9780875161686 www.devorss.com, 45.

122 Matthew 5:21–22 TLB.

123 Matthew 5:44b.

124 *Dowling, The Aquarian Gospel of Jesus the Christ*, 26.

125 *The Word of the Lord and the Spirit of the Lord*, Vol. 33. New Britain, CT: Scriptural Research & Publishing Co., 2005, 256–258.

126 Matthew 18:21b–22.

127 Matthew 5:23–25a.

128 Worcester, *Physiological Correspondences*, 106.

129 Isaiah 5:11.

130 1 Peter 2:1–2.

131 Proverbs 19:11 TLB.

132 1 John 1:9.

133 Deuteronomy 29:18.

134 Acts 8:22–23.

135 Ephesians 4:31–32 TLB.

136 Hebrews 12:15.

137 Luke 6:37b.

138 Luke 6:37a TLB.

139 Clayman, *The Human Body*, 230.

140 Worcester, *Physiological Correspondences*, 114, 120–121.

141 Benjamin F. Miller and Claire Brackman Keane. *Encyclopedia and Dictionary of Medicine and Nursing.* Oxford, UK: W. B. Saunders/Elsevier, 1972, 162.

142 Lydia Temoshok and Henry Drehr. *Type C Connection.* New York: Penguin Random House, 1992, 24.

143 Ephesians 4:26–27 TLB.

144 *The Word of the Lord,* Vol. 33, 255.

145 Parker, *The Human Body Book*, 146.

146 Psalm 39:4–6a, 11.

147 Proverbs 31:30.

148 Galatians 5:26.

149 Psalm 119:165.

150 Genesis 2:23b.

151 Genesis 2:24b, 5:2.

152 Emanuel Swedenborg, *Conjugial Love*, Translated by Samuel M. Warren and Louis H. Tafel, New York: Swedenborg Foundation, 1971, 60 n.50.

153 Matthew 18:19b, 20b.

154 Swedenborg, *Conjugial Love,* 60–61 n. 50.

155 Matthew 19:5b–6.

156 *The Word of the Lord,* Vol. 12, 6–7.

157 1 Peter 3:7.

158 1 Peter 3:7 TLB.

159 Matthew 5:27–28.

160 Genesis 20:3b.

161 Genesis 20:6–7.

162 Genesis 20:17–18.

163 *The Holy Spirit Teachings of God's Original Intention.* New Britain, CT: Scriptural Research & Publishing Co., 3.

164 Swedenborg, *Heaven and Hell,* Translated by George Dole. West Chester, PA: Swedenborg Foundation, 2000, 267 n. 332.

165 Isaiah 66:9a, c.

166 Ecclesiastes 11:5.

167 Psalm 37:4–5.

168 1 Timothy 2:15b.

169 *The Word of the Lord,* Vol. 21, 181–182.

170 Parker, *The Human Body Book*, 227.

171 Hay, *You Can Heal Your Life*, 170.

172 Galatians 5:16–17, 19, 21b, 24.

173 1 Thessalonians 4:3.

174 Galatians 6:8.

175 Jeremiah 3:13, 14a, 15.

176 2 Timothy 2:22.

177 Proverbs 6:25–29.

178 1 Corinthians 6:18–20 TLB.

179 Swedenborg, *Heaven and Hell*, Translated by George Dole, 350–351 n. 462b [2, 8].

180 Joshua 7:12a, c.

181 Zechariah 4:10a.

182 John 10:1b, 8a, 10.

183 2 Timothy 3: 2a, 5.

184 *The Word of the Lord*, Vol. 56, 88–89.

185 Swedenborg, *Heaven and Hell*, Translated by George Dole, 94 n.10.

186 Swedenborg, *Heaven and Hell*, Translated by George Dole, 351 n. 463.

187 Swedenborg, *Heaven and Hell*, 124 n. 231.

188 Proverbs 3:9–10.

189 Proverbs 3:27–28, TLB.

190 Proverbs 21:25–26 TLB.

191 Mark 9:43–44 TLB.

192 Ephesians 4:28.

193 Luke 6: 29b–33a TLB.

194 1 Thessalonians 4:11–12.

195 1 Thessalonians 4:11a–12 TLB.

196 Malachi 3:8, 10.

197 Parker, *The Human Body Book*, 92.

198 Worcester, *Physiological Correspondences*, 302.

199 Matthew 13:14b–15.

200 John 9:39b–41.

201 Psalm 119:130.

202 *God Can Heal You*, 8.

203 Proverbs 14:16 TLB.

204 Proverbs 13:16 TLB.

205 Deuteronomy 32:29.

206 Proverbs 28:22.

207 Proverbs 22:3 TLB.

208 *God Can Heal You*, 9.

209 Matthew 6:23–24, 31a, 31c–34 TLB.

210 Matthew 6:19–21.

211 Proverbs 12:15.

212 Proverbs 3:7–8.

213 Matthew 7:3–5.

214 1 Corinthians 13:5b TLB.

215 Isaiah 52:7a.

216 *God Can Heal You*, 8.

217 Psalm 91:11–12.

218 Numbers 22:32b.

219 *The Word of the Lord*, Vol. 12, 8–9.

220 Exodus 23:20–22.

221 Isaiah 30:21.

222 Proverbs 28:26.

223 Psalm 119:101, 105.

224 Proverbs 3:21b–23.

225 Proverbs 25:17, 19.

226 Hebrews 12:13–14.

227 Psalm 37:23, 26.

228 2 Corinthians 9:6b–7.

229 2 Corinthians 9:7–9, 11–13 TLB.

230 Proverbs 11:24–25 TLB.

231 Luke 6:38, 30, 34–35.

232 Genesis 3:4b.

233 *The Holy Spirit Teachings*, 7.

234 Isaiah 26:3.

235 *Dowling, Aquarian Gospel of Jesus the Christ*, back cover, John 16:12–13.

236 John 8:44a, c, 45, 46b–47.

237 1 John 4:6.

238 Jeremiah 17:9–10.

239 Deuteronomy 19:15–17a, 18–19 TLB.

240 Luke 8:18, 17.

241 Proverbs 25:18 TLB.

242 *Tests of Character*. New Britain, CT: Scriptural Research & Publishing Co., 3.

243 Hebrews 4:12–13.

244 Myss, *Anatomy of the Spirit*, 221.

245 Emanuel Swedenborg. *Way of Wisdom: Meditations on Love and Service*. West Chester, PA: Chrysalis Books, 1999, 23.

246 2 Timothy 4:3–4.

247 1 John 2:4–6.

248 *Walk with the Proverbs*. New Britain, CT: Truth Center, Inc., 1993, 29.

249 Deuteronomy 6:6–7 TLB.

250 *Walk with the Proverbs*, 26.

251 *Walk with the Proverbs*, 19.

252 *Walk with the Proverbs*, 40.

253 *Walk with the Proverbs*, 27.

254 *Walk with the Proverbs*, 21.

255 *Walk with the Proverbs*, 24.

256 Exodus 23:1–3 TLB.

257 *Walk with the Proverbs*, 23.

258 Leviticus 19:11, 12a, 16–17 TLB.

259 Psalm 15:1–3a, 4, 5b TLB.

260 Proverbs 11:12–13 TLB.

261 Ephesians 4:25 TLB.

262 Matthew 5:34b.

263 Matthew 5:37 TLB.

264 Ecclesiastes 5:4–5 TLB.

265 Job 32:8.

266 Parker, *The Human Body Book*, 132.

267 Proverbs 3:13a, 18.

268 Norman Cousins. *Anatomy of an Illness as Perceived by the Patient.* New York: W.W. Norton & Company, 1979, 84.

269 Parker, *The Human Body Book*, 139–142.

270 *God Can Heal You,* 4.

271 1 Timothy 4:16 TLB.

272 Isaiah 55:2.

273 Hebrews 13:5.

274 Ephesians 5:3, 5 TLB.

275 1 Timothy 6:17–19 TLB.

276 Mark 4:18–19.

277 Luke 10:5.

278 Mark 8:36–37.

279 Luke 12:15.

280 Dispenza, *Breaking the Habit of Being Yourself,* 162–163.

281 Timothy 6:6.

282 1 Timothy 6:7–10 TLB.

283 Swedenborg, *Heaven and Hell,* Translated by George Dole, 449 n. 598.

284 Philippians 4:11b–13.

285 Dowling, *The Aquarian Gospel of Jesus the Christ,* 41–42.

Bibliography

Allen, James. *As a Man Thinketh*. Camarillo, CA: DeVorss & Company.

Clayman, Charles B. *The Human Body*. Philadelphia, PA: DK Publishing/ Penguin Random House, 1995.

Cousins, Norman. *Anatomy of an Illness as Perceived by the Patient*. New York: W. W. Norton & Company, Inc., 1979.

Dispenza, Joe. *Breaking the Habit of Being Yourself*. Carlsbad, CA: Hay House Inc., 2012.

Dowling, Levi. *The Aquarian Gospel of Jesus the Christ.*. Camarillo, CA: DeVorss & Company, 2006.

God Can Heal You. New Britain, CT: Scriptural Research Co. Inc., 1987.

Hay, Louise. *You Can Heal Your Life*. Carlsbad, CA: Hay House Inc., 2004.

Levi. *The Aquarian Gospel.*Miller, Benjamin F., and Claire Brackman Keane. *Encyclopedia and Dictionary of Medicine and Nursing*. Oxford, UK: W. B. Saunders Co./Elsevier Ltd., 1972.

Myss, Caroline. *Anatomy of the Spirit*. New York: MJF Books/Penguin Random House, 1996.

Parker, Steve. *The Human Body Book*. New York: DK Publishing/Penguin Random House, 2007.

Peale, Norman Vincent. *The Power of Positive Thinking*. New York: FIRESIDE, a Division of Simon & Schuster, Inc., 2008.

Swedenborg, Emmanuel. *Conjugial Love.*Translated by Samuel M. Warren and Louis H. Tafel. New York: Swedenborg Foundation Inc., 1971.

Swedenborg, Emmanuel. *Heaven and Hell*. Translated by George Dole. West Chester, PA: Swedenborg Foundation, 2000.

Swedenborg, Emmanuel. *Heaven and Hell,* Standard Edition. Translated by A. C. Ager. New York: Swedenborg Foundation Inc., 1978.

Swedenborg, Emmanuel. *Way of Wisdom: Meditations on Love and Service.* Edited by Grant R. Schnarr and Erik J. Buss. West Chester, PA: Chrysalis Books, 1999.

Temshok, Lydia, and Henry Drehr. *The Type C Connection.* New York: Penguin Random House LLC, 1992.

Tests of Character. New Britain, CT: Scriptural Research and Publishing Co., Inc.

The Holy Spirit Teachings of God's Original Intention. New Britain, CT: Scriptural Research & Publishing Co., Inc.

The King James Study Bible. Nashville, TN: Thomas Nelson Publishers, 1988.

The Living Bible. Carol Stream, IL: Tyndale House Publishers, Inc., 1971.

The Word of the Lord and the Spirit of the Lord. Vol. 12. New Britain, CT: Scriptural Research & Publishing Co., Inc., 2003.

The Word of the Lord and the Spirit of the Lord. Vol. 21. New Britain, CT: Scriptural Research & Publishing Co., Inc., 2003.

The Word of the Lord and the Spirit of the Lord. Vol. 33. New Britain, CT: Scriptural Research & Publishing Co., Inc., 2005.

The Word of the Lord and the Spirit of the Lord. Vol. 56. New Britain, CT: Scriptural Research & Publishing Co., Inc., 2009.

Walk with the Proverbs (a polyglot). New Britain, CT: The Truth Center, Inc., 1993.

Worcester, John. *Physiological Correspondences.* Bryn Athyn, PA: Swedenborg Scientific Association, 1987.

Wright, Henry. *A More Excellent Way To Be in Health.* New Kensington, PA: Whitaker House, 2009.

Index

H

Habit xiii, xvii, 19, 21, 27, 28, 32, 46, 70, 71, 82, 90, 125, 138, 141, 158, 174, 180, 181

Hair 89, 91, 113

Hand problems/injuries 117

Hands 9, 15, 17, 28, 56, 57, 58, 59, 70, 71, 102, 109, 112, 113, 116, 117, 118, 124, 126, 127, 128

Left hand 9, 117

Right hand 9, 56, 57, 117, 127

Hannah ix, 101

Hate (red) 21, 25, 26, 62, 78, 79, 85, 88, 122, 128, 146

Headaches 152

Heal xiv, 15, 16, 19, 21, 44, 58, 59, 60, 67, 69, 105, 113, 120, 121, 122, 125, 151, 153, 161, 175, 177, 178, 180, 181

Healthy 15, 19, 29, 34, 35, 39, 59, 65, 69, 85, 107

Hearing 2, 120, 135, 136, 140, 141, 142, 143, 152

Heart vii, xiii, 3, 4, 9, 14, 15, 17, 18, 23, 25, 26, 27, 28, 29, 30, 31, 32, 33, 34, 35, 40, 41, 42, 44, 50, 53, 58, 66, 67, 68, 74, 79, 83, 84, 86, 96, 99, 100, 103, 104, 107, 111, 120, 121, 123, 127, 128, 129, 136, 137, 140, 142, 145, 151, 161

Heartbreak 15

Heartburn 45, 46

Heart problems 25, 30, 31

Heaven xiii, 1, 4, 7, 16, 22, 25, 31, 44, 49, 52, 54, 66, 81, 95, 96, 102, 104, 111, 115, 116, 117, 118, 123, 140, 142, 150, 155, 157, 158, 174, 177, 178, 180, 181

Hell 31, 78, 102, 111, 112, 115, 116, 117, 158, 174, 177, 178, 180, 181

Hepatitis 82, 83

Hereditary xiii, xv, 27, 28, 81, 102, 103, 104, 112, 123, 141

Heredity 55, 61, 87, 123

High blood pressure 32

Hope xvii, 59, 60, 61, 121, 126, 130, 137, 161, 162

Humble 16, 71, 154

Humility 71

Husband ix, 26, 65, 96, 98, 99, 100, 101

Hypocrisy 35, 42, 43, 83

Hypocrites 124

I

Idolatry 23, 27, 30, 34

Idols 25, 27, 30, 32, 154

Illness xv, xvi, xvii, 10, 15, 16, 27, 28, 35, 52, 61, 78, 98, 99, 106, 134, 136, 152, 161, 162, 180, 181

Images 9, 23, 25, 28, 30, 34, 65, 89, 115, 119

Immune system xiii, 20, 80, 86, 87, 88, 98, 152

Impressions 67, 69, 141, 151, 153

Infertility 99, 100, 101, 102, 105

Inflammation 143, 153

Inflexibility 70, 153

Iniquity 25, 34, 84, 89, 106

Injuries 19, 117, 126

Insomnia 54, 55

Inspiration ix, xvii, 4, 31, 66, 67, 70, 71, 85, 86, 126, 149, 150, 151, 152, 154, 155, 160, 161

Intelligence 23, 45, 72, 145

J

Job 14, 19, 26, 29, 33, 41, 53, 56, 69, 81, 82, 83, 85, 86, 87, 103, 114, 136, 159, 174, 175, 180

CPSIA information can be obtained
at www.ICGtesting.com
Printed in the USA
BVHW03s0333220218
508758BV00001B/1/P

9 781973 608226